THE MULE TRAIN

A Journey of Hope Remembered

THE MULE TRAIN

A Journey of Hope Remembered

ROLAND L. FREEMAN

Edited by
David B. Levine

RUTLEDGE HILL PRESS ®

Nashville, Tennessee

Published by Rutledge Hill Press®, 211 Seventh Avenue North, Nashville, Tennessee 37219

Distributed in Canada by H. B. Fenn & Company, Ltd., 34 Nixon Road, Bolton, Ontario L7E 1W2. Distributed in Australia by The Five Mile Press Pty., Ltd., 22 Summit Road, Noble Park, Victoria 3174. Distributed in New Zealand by Tandem Press, 2 Rugby Road, Birkenhead, Auckland 10. Distributed in the United Kingdom by Verulam Publishing, Ltd., 152a Park Street Lane, Park Street, St. Albans, Hertfordshire AL2 2AU.

Cover and book design by Harriette Bateman
Photography by Roland L. Freeman

The following publishers have generously given their permission to use extended quotations from copyrighted works:

Ferris, William R. "Mules in the South." In *Mules and Mississippi, edited by* Patti Carr Black. Jackson, Mississippi, 1980. Reprinted courtesy of the author and the Mississippi Department of Archives and History.

Franklin, John Hope, and Alfred A. Moss Jr. *From Slavery to Freedom: A History of African Americans*. 7th ed. New York: McGraw-Hill, 1994.

Hampton, Henry, and Steve Fayer. *Voices of Freedom: An Oral History of the Civil Rights Movement from the 1950s through 1980s*. Blackside, 1990.

New York Times Copyright © 1968 by The New York Times Co. Reprinted by permission.

Walker, Margaret. *This Is My Century: New and Collected Poems*. Athens and London: University of Georgia Press, 1989. Selection reprinted with permission from Margaret Walker Alexander.

Young, Andrew. *An Easy Burden*. New York: Harper Collins Publishers, 1996.

Information about the exhibit:

The national touring exhibit of *The Mule Train: A Journey of Hope Remembered* will remain available for bookings indefinitely. For information, contact The Group for Cultural Documentation (TGCD); 117 Ingraham Street, NW; Washington, D.C. 20011; fax (202) 829-6814; E-mail freeroland@aol.com.

ISBN 1-55853-660-4
Library of Congress Cataloging-in-Publication Data available

Printed in the United States of America
1 2 3 4 5 6 7 8 9—00 99 98

CONTENTS

ACKNOWLEDGMENTS

This project would not have been possible without the support, assistance, and guidance of a vast network of people who provided me with the resources to bring it to fruition. Under difficult time constraints, they went the extra miles—lending their hands as needed and going far beyond any reasonable call of duty.

I would first like to extend a special thanks to David B. Levine. To edit a book such as this takes special skills of understanding and collaboration. I appreciate David for his friendship, commitment, and tireless energy in helping complete this book, and his unfailing insistence on clarity and rigor—without it, publication would not have been possible. Also vital were the contributions of Judith H. Katz, a wonderful friend and a board member of The Group for Cultural Documentation (TGCD), Keisha Abney (my key assistant) and Carmen Clad-Jones who helped with research and materials preparation, and my wife, Marcia, who contributes significantly to everything I do.

The people of Marks, Mississippi, provided the impetus for this project. I felt I had no choice but to respond to the combination of Hilliard Lackey's suggestion of a 30th Anniversary Mule Train Celebration, the diligent work put forth by the local Steering Committee, and the grassroots effort and enthusiasm this reflected. I especially would like to thank Bertha Johnson Luster who first informed me about the celebration and also contributed her own recollections to the book, and Samuel McCray, the Marks liaison for U.S. Congressperson Bennie Thompson, who kept me informed as things developed.

I owe a special thanks to Willie Bolden, John Cashin, Lee Dora Collins, Myrna Copeland, Jean Smith Freas, and Lydia McKinnon, who shared and discussed their stories and reflections. They, along with the others cited in the text, helped me develop my historical and personal perspective on the Poor People's Campaign in general, and the Mule Train in particular.

I am greatly indebted to all of the photographers—Bernie Boston, Dennis Brack, Robert Burchette, Brig Cabe, Ken Heinen, Steven Northup, Burke Uzzle, and Ernest Withers—who contributed their images to build a body of work that would do justice to the telling of the Mule Train story.

I would also like to acknowledge the people who helped in providing contacts and clarifying background information: Sheryll D. Cashin, Jim Coles, Joseph Elbert, Jean Fox-Alston, Regina Johnson, Lynn Kneedler, Bill McAfee, Marilyn Sanders, and Chrissy Wilson and others at the Mississippi Department of Archives and History.

Finally, I would like to thank the following for their financial contributions to TGCD, without which the touring exhibit, *The Mule Train: A Journey of Hope Remembered*, would not have been possible: The W. K. Kellogg Foundation, The Rockefeller Foundation, the Turner Foundation, and Dr. Eleanor Foster Ott, a close friend and benefactor.

Roland L. Freeman on assignment with the Mule Train

MARKS, MISSISSIPPI, MAY 1968

INTRODUCTION

The Mule Train
A Journey of Hope Remembered—An Overview

WHY THIS BOOK AT THIS TIME

On September 16, 1997, civil rights activist Bertha Johnson Luster called me from Marks, Mississippi. I had first met Ms. Luster and her six children in May 1968 on the Mule Train, part of the Southern Christian Leadership Conference's (SCLC) Poor People's Campaign. She said she had located my business card in an old box of civil rights memorabilia, and I was overjoyed to hear from her. I got excited when she told me that people in Marks were planning a 30th Anniversary Mule Train Celebration. Of the many caravans of poor people that came to Washington, D.C., from the four corners of the United States, this was probably the most dramatic—and the only one not made up of buses, cars, or vans.

When I hung up the telephone, I remembered what led me to Marks in the late 1960s. After hearing Dr. Martin Luther King Jr.'s "I Have a Dream" speech in 1963, I was inspired to become a photographer and committed myself to the documentation of black culture. With no formal training I began to freelance full-time and also increased my direct participation in civil rights demonstrations, both in and around Washington and farther south. I recalled how when Dr. King was murdered in Memphis, Tennessee, on April 4, 1968, a shock wave went through America and a cloud of smoke hung over the capital as Washington burned.

By month's end, I had joined hundreds of other volunteers committed to the success of Dr. King's last effort, the Poor People's Campaign, and found myself part of the SCLC's documentation and communication corps. After covering some early campaign activities in Washington in late April, I remembered traveling to Memphis for the send-off for the southern caravan. By early May I was in Marks, Mississippi, assigned the daunting task of photographing the Mule Train as it journeyed to Washington, D.C. Feeling very much the novice, I was initially intimidated by my assignment, but with each succeeding day, as I saw the courage, strength, and wisdom of people on the front lines in the struggle for social justice, my fear dissipated and was replaced with commitment; I knew there was nowhere else on earth that I would prefer to be.

Now it was thirty years later, and Ms. Luster, Marks, and those heady days of 1968 had reentered my life. I went to my files and found notes and images from the Mule Train and was saddened by the reminders that I wasn't nearly as good a photographer then as I am now. I often didn't know what I was doing technically, was unfamiliar with the context in which I was working, was using a couple of old cameras with defective lenses and didn't document my work as thoroughly as I've since learned to do. In short, I remembered that I often felt as though I was hanging on by my gut instincts! At the same time, I was pleased to see that despite my inexperience I had a range of good shots that spoke true to the experience along with a nearly complete roster of the people who had been on the Mule Train and transcripts of several interviews.

Looking at the photographs, I was suddenly overcome. I broke down and cried. By the time I collected myself, I realized that an exhibit of these materials should be part of the Mule Train Celebration; they would help show what the experience was actually like. I decided to participate directly and sent a letter to Ms. Luster volunteering to curate such an exhibit. My thought was for a show that, while centered on my own work, would include that of other Poor People's Campaign photographers and incorporate a new field research component to supplement and update what I had available. Ms. Luster encouraged me to take on this effort and on behalf of the 30th Anniversary Steering Committee[1] and invited me to Marks, Mississippi, to attend an October planning meeting, at which the exhibit was officially incorporated into the May 1998 celebration.

Though I had worked extensively in Mississippi

---

[1] The ten members of this committee were Helen Ingram (president), Shirley French, Willie French, Robert L. Jackson, Charles Langford, Bertha Johnson Luster, Bernestine Humphrey McCray, Samuel McCray, (Ms.) DeMarche Robinzine, and Larry Smith.

since the Mule Train, this was the first time in thirty years that I'd returned to Marks. The town had undergone a cosmetic facelift, but it seemed to me that its economics hadn't changed dramatically in the intervening years—and according to the 1960 U.S. census, Quitman County, of which Marks is the county seat, was then the country's poorest. What clearly had changed, and dramatically, was the role blacks were now playing; Marks had a young African-American mayor, an integrated Board of County Supervisors, and Representative Bennie Thompson, an African-American U.S. congress-person.

Hilliard Lackey, a professor of history at Mississippi's Jackson State University, originally conceived the 30th Anniversary Celebration, and key to his thinking was that such an event might stimulate economic development in Marks. The Steering Committee intends the celebration to be an annual event, eventually including a permanent museum that would function as a center for research about the Poor People's Campaign and other local history.

As of this writing (March 1998), the inaugural Mule Train Celebration is scheduled for May 22-24, 1998, Memorial Day weekend, also traditionally the time for Marks's high school graduation and homecoming. The committee anticipates this timing to encourage broad participation. Marks's Quitman County High School will serve as the headquarters for the three days of events and the venue for the exhibit.

Field research and fund-raising, supported by The Group for Cultural Documentation (TGCD),[2] began almost immediately after my phone call from Ms. Luster and is still underway. After its showing in Marks, the exhibit, also called *The Mule Train: A Journey of Hope Remembered*, will initiate an ongoing tour, with stops already scheduled for the Martin Luther King Jr. National Historic Site Visitor's Center (Atlanta, GA), the Smith Robertson Museum (Jackson, MS), Mississippi Cultural Crossroads (Port Gibson, MS), and the Smithsonian Institution (Washington, D.C.)

Early in the process of conceptualizing this project, I realized its results could be shaped into a worthwhile book, which would provide a lasting tribute to the Mule Train, accessible where the exhibit would not be. I contacted my publisher, Lawrence

Stone, who had worked closely with me in 1996 to publish my earlier work, *A Communion of the Spirits: African-American Quilters, Preservers, and Their Stories*.[3] We agreed to develop this book as an additional element of the 30th Anniversary Celebration of the Mule Train.

The most challenging aspect of the effort would prove to be to have it ready and in Marks for the May 1998 celebration. To do this, Lawrence and I agreed to the following: he would have a full text and all photographs in his hands by no later than early March 1998; that text would have been fully developed and edited in collaboration with David B. Levine, who had worked closely with me on *A Communion of the Spirits*, and Lawrence and I would work closely together on the book design. This translated into only a five-month time frame between our initial conversation and the due date for final copy. We had only a brief period of time in which to track down and reinterview some of the people initially involved, and we had to limit the range of our literature searches and original media coverage in order to meet the deadline.

As I moved ahead, aware of the challenge of accurately portraying and preserving this historic event of thirty years ago, I became increasingly angry and frustrated as I realized how little of the extensive field documentation—mine and others, both photographic and textual—was actually available. Much of it had disappeared either in the chaotic communications of the campaign itself; or when temporary operation headquarters in Washington closed down; or over the intervening years as those involved moved on or passed on; or in the Smithsonian's cataloguing and storage of various gifts of memorabilia. This further reduced the amounts of historical information we could consult and our options as to what to include.

We decided to focus the available time on locating and involving the other photographers and on developing the primary materials we already had by recontacting individuals who had participated in the Mule Train. This implied that we would rely extensively on few sources, piecing the narrative together by incorporating, linking, and clarifying a limited amount of primary material. Related to this is the fact that virtually no original caption material was available for most of the photographs. Therefore, as you'll see, though each photograph has been generally identified, key data about who, what, and where are often somewhat sketchy.[4]

[2] TGCD is a publicly funded organization located in Washington, D.C., of which I am founder and president. Established in 1991, its purpose is to increase awareness, understanding, and appreciation of the nature, continuity, vitality, and significance of our country's cultural traditions. We do this by supporting their preservation and documentation within and among communities, and by developing deeper awareness and understanding of the strength and value provided by community and national cultural diversity.

[3] Roland L. Freeman, *A Communion of the Spirits: African-American Quilters, Preservers, and Their Stories*. (Nashville, TN: Rutledge Hill Press, 1996).

[4] An early compilation of some of the material in this book appeared in Vol. 4, No. 1, the Spring 1998 *Southern Cultures*, a journal published by the University of North Carolina, Chapel Hill.

THE PHOTOGRAPHERS WHOSE WORK IS INCLUDED

These conditions also impacted my choice of work to include from others covering the Poor People's Campaign. Although there were numerous photographers involved whose work I respected, I limited myself to those few who could provide material from aspects of the campaign I missed, whom I could quickly track down, and whose photographs and authorizations were readily available. While I regret how limited a sample they are of the wonderful work done during that time period, I'm pleased and excited about the individuals who are included, and I am indebted to them for their willingness to be part of this important tribute.

Bernie Boston was then head of the Photography Department at the *Washington Star*, a now defunct newspaper. He covered the Mule Train between its arrival in northern Virginia and its entrance into Resurrection City. He is now retired and lives in Virginia.

Dennis Brack was then a Washington, D.C.-based photographer, working for Black Star, a photo agency in New York. Brack traveled with the Washington press corps to Memphis, Tennessee, to cover the send-off for the southern caravan. This included the march and ceremonies related to the unveiling of a plaque that commemorated the assassination of Dr. King. Brack is still part of the Washington press corps and affiliated with Black Star.

Robert Burchette was then a *Washington Post* staff photographer assigned to the Poor People's Campaign. He retired about fifteen years ago.

Brig Cabe was then an SCLC staff photographer working out of their Atlanta headquarters. He traveled with Dr. King during the winter of 1968 while preparations were under way for the Poor People's Campaign. He later took a position at the *Washington Star* and is now freelancing in the Washington, D.C., area.

Ken Heinen, a native Washingtonian, was then a staff photographer for the *Evening Star*, an afternoon newspaper. He photographed the Poor People's Campaign from the arrival of the Mule Train in northern Virginia through the destruction of Resurrection City. He is now a freelance photographer in the Washington, D.C., area. When I asked Heinen about the experience, he reflected:

> Later that day, I gained new insights while walking along with the Mule Train as it moved slowly through the streets of Washington. I heard bull horns blaring harsh words from the leadership, but I saw desperation mixed with determination in the eyes of the people riding in those wagons. I sensed the fear blended with the

hope they were feeling. These appeared to be just plain folks who had swallowed their pride while gathering enough courage to show the nation their rage. They had arrived in Washington unsure of what to expect, but had come fully committed to their cause. I did not forget these images while documenting the strife that followed, nor throughout the anguished days and restless nights of Resurrection City.

Stephen Northup was then a *Washington Post* staff photographer. He photographed the Mule Train entering Washington and covered Resurrection City throughout the summer. He later served as head of the photography department of a newspaper in Santa Fe, New Mexico and is now retired.

Burke Uzzle was then a New York-based photographer and a member of Magnum, an international photo agency. He is now a freelance photographer based in Florida.

Ernest Withers was then a Memphis-based freelance photographer affiliated with the *Tri-State Defender*. He photographed the Civil Rights movement in Memphis and Mississippi. He still lives in Memphis, in semiretirement.

There are also a couple of images by unidentified photographers provided by United Press International (UPI). All photographs that are not otherwise specified are by Roland L. Freeman.

TWO PERSONAL NOTES: MISSISSIPPI AND MULES

Two personal dimensions clarify why it was so important to me to respond to the planning under way in Marks; to put aside all my other projects and harness my, and others', energy and resources for the extensive push necessary to be part of the 30th Anniversary Mule Train Celebration. The first has to do with Mississippi. Let me start with a story.

Burke Uzzle was one of my mentors when I first became a photographer. I remember clearly how in one of our earliest sessions he asked me to identify my ten worst fears as to what I might encounter as a photographer. Near the top of my list was working in the Deep South, particularly in Mississippi. Burke also told me that I would be a successful photographer only if I confronted and overcame each of these fears. My experience with the Mule Train provided me opportunities for both.

I think it was more than twenty-five years earlier, when I was about seven years old, that I first heard about Mississippi. The women who frequently gathered in my grandmother's kitchen were talking about "hard times down South." Someone said that of all the southern states things were worst in Mississippi; they were so bad that they dared not go back, even for funerals. Over subsequent years I heard countless people mention "hard times Mississippi," so much so that when I was twelve, and moved from the city of Baltimore to a farm in southern Maryland, I had a lot of mixed feelings. To my youthful mind, this meant that I was going "down South," and I prayed real hard that it wouldn't be as bad as Mississippi.

While living in Charles County, Maryland, I came under the tutelage of Jeannetta Chase, an elderly cousin who was an educator. On my thirteenth birthday, she gave me several books, among them Margaret Walker's collection of poems, *For My People*. Of all the poems in this book, the one that intrigued me most was "Delta." Cousin Jeannetta explained to me that the Delta was this vast, rich farmland near the lower end of the Mississippi River where thousands of black folks were taken during slavery to raise cotton, rice, and sugarcane. She also said that even though slavery had been over for almost one hundred years, most of us in the Delta weren't much better off than before freedom came—she called sharecropping just another form of slavery. Later, during restless nights on the Mule Train, I often found solace rereading this poem. Being on the land and among the folk of whom Walker was speaking, I reached a new understanding of her words.

Here are a few excerpts from "Delta.[5]

I am a child of the valley.
Mud and muck and misery of lowlands
are on thin tracks of my feet.
. . . . . .

O valley of my moaning brothers!
Valley of my sorrowing sisters!
Valley of lost forgotten men.
. . . . . .

Here in this valley of cotton and cane and banana
    wharves
we labor.
Our mothers and fathers labored before us
here in this low valley.
. . . . . .

We tend the crop and gather the harvest
but not for ourselves do we labor,
not for ourselves do we sweat and starve and spend
under these mountains we dare not claim,
here on this earth we dare not claim,
here by the river we dare not claim.
Yet we are an age of years in this valley;
yet we are bound till death to this valley.
. . . . . .

Out of a deep slumber truth rides upon us
and makes us restless and wakeful
and full of a hundred unfulfilled dreams of today;
our blood eats through our veins with the terrible
    destruction
of radium in our bones and rebellion in our brains
and we wish no longer to rest.

As you can see, I brought a lot of baggage with me to this assignment. By its completion, I had repacked those bags with love, understanding, and admiration of the Delta's people and their struggles. In the years since, Mississippi has become my adopted state and the one to which I have most often returned for both work and rejuvenation—though never without echoes of my childhood fears and concerns.

The second personal dimension relates to how horses and wagons are in my blood. Though I'd planned on remaining in Washington to cover Poor People's Campaign activities here, I jumped at the chance to document the Mule Train. You see, in Baltimore, where I grew up, there was a tradition called "arabbing"—the selling of fruits and vegetables from horse- and mule-drawn wagons.[6] I was the fourth generation of arabbers in my family, and from when I was seven until I was twelve, I spent much of my time on those wagons and in the stables caring for the horses and mules. Of course, I had heard about "40 acres and a mule" and was interested in knowing more about how mules were used in the South. More important—like a little kid—I was intrigued at the idea of traveling almost a thousand miles in wagons drawn by animals whose speed and endurance I thought I already knew from personal experience.

THE LAYOUT OF THE BOOK

The book is divided into two major parts. The first part, "Images of the Journey," tells the Mule Train story through photographs accompanied by brief extracts. These are presented chronologically, from the conceptualization of the Poor People's Campaign in late 1967 through the close down of Resurrection City in late June 1968.

The second part, "A Narrative of the Journey," focuses on the Mule Train while incorporating an overview of the broader context of the Poor People's Campaign. It covers the same period as the photographs, from the SCLC's strategic planning during the last months of Dr. King's life through the

---

[5] Margaret Walker's, *This Is My Century: New and Collected Poems.* (Athens and London: University of Georgia Press, 1989), 15-20.

[6] Further details on "arabbing," the practice of selling fruits and vegetables from horse-drawn wagons in Baltimore and other cities, and on my childhood, split between Sandtown, a Baltimore community, and Charles County, Maryland, can be found in my books *The Arabbers of Baltimore*, (Centreville, MD: Tidewater Publishers, 1998) and *A Communion of the Spirits*, cited earlier.....

suspension of campaign activities in mid-1968. The emphasis is on the Mule Train itself—its people, their preparations, and their voices, then and now, reflecting on what occurred and its meaning. The first part of the narrative draws on interviews with Mule Train participants and organizers from Marks and nearby communities, conversations with then members of the SCLC's leadership, and contemporary local and national newspaper coverage. The second half includes extensive comments from seven individuals—two Mule Train participants from Marks, Bertha Johnson Luster and Lee Dora Collins; three volunteer organizers from Alabama, Joan Cashin, Myrna Copeland, and John Cashin; Wagon Master Willie Bolden; and Jean Smith Freas, a television journalist at the time who provided extensive Mule Train coverage—to give us a feel for the lives and experiences of persons who were directly involved.

The appendix provides a reasonably complete roster of more than 100 people who rode on the Mule Train through Mississippi and Alabama.

I invite you to join me in the following pages on the journey of the Mule Train with participants who courageously provided a living statement to our nation and the world about the struggles of those caught in poverty in 1968 and now. This book is dedicated to their efforts and honors the hope that they will not be forgotten.

PART ONE

Images of the Journey

A mother and her four children at home

MARKS, MISSISSIPPI, EARLY MAY 1968

Marian Wright Edelman
WASHINGTON, D.C., LATE APRIL 1968

IN 1967, DR. MARTIN LUTHER KING JR. was keenly aware of the importance of broadening the focus of the Civil Rights movement. He now saw poverty as the key issue and knew that arousing the nation's conscience about it required an approach encompassing all of America's poor. It was in this context that in September 1967, he met with Marian Wright (later Edelman), an African-American attorney, then the director of the Mississippi office of the NAACP Legal Defense and Education Fund. Ms. Wright was urging the Southern Christian Leadership Conference (SCLC) to adopt a focus on employment and job training using such strategies as demonstrations, sit-ins, and fasts in Washington, D.C. These activities would continue until the problems of chronic unemployment and the related plight of the poor were addressed at the national level. Ms. Wright's ideas were explored in the meeting and were the seeds from which Dr. King grew the Poor People's Campaign over the following weeks.

Dr. Martin Luther King Jr. visiting a church during the planning of the Poor People's Campaign

IN MARKS, MISSISSIPPI, I well remember, we visited a day-care center. And Dr. King was moved to tears there. There was one apple, and they took this apple and cut it into four pieces for four hungry waiting students. And when Dr. King saw that, and that is all that they had for lunch, he actually ended up crying. The tears came streaming down his cheek. And he had to leave the room.

Rev. Ralph Abernathy

ECONOMICALLY, LITTLE HAD CHANGED by the 1960s: poverty and hunger were rampant; in rural areas, sharecropping was still the rule; jobs were scarce and wages inadequate; and structural and institutional changes were cosmetic at best. For the Poor People's Campaign, thousands of demonstrators would come to Washington from all around the country. Significant numbers of them would live in temporary housing constructed for that purpose, and they would demonstrate and petition the government for an "economic bill of rights." SCLC staff fanned out across the country meeting with and organizing poor Hispanic, Native American, white, and African-American communities for participation in this new movement that would transcend race while nonviolently seeking social and economic justice.

Child at the Mule Train preparation site
MARKS, MISSISSIPPI, EARLY MAY 1968

Children playing in an alley in Chinatown

SAN FRANCISCO, CALIFORNIA, AUGUST 1972

Mexican-Americans at home in the Southwest

NEAR BROWNSVILLE, TEXAS, OCTOBER 1978

A woman and her granddaughter in Appalachia

BARWICK, KENTUCKY, OCTOBER 1978

Powwow on a Native American reservation

<small>Niagara Falls, New York, September 1978</small>

A man representing the elderly poor
at a U.S. Congressional hearing on
Capitol Hill

<small>Washington, D.C., late April 1968</small>

DR. MARTIN LUTHER KING JR. was assassinated in Memphis on April 4, 1968, in the midst of final planning for the Poor People's Campaign. It took the SCLC but a moment to renew its commitment to moving ahead with the campaign, believing firmly that would have been Dr. King's insistence. The Poor People's Committee of one hundred attended to both lobbying and implementation. Although they were rushed and many details that were left unattended would later haunt the campaign, Dr. Abernathy formally announced on April 19 that all would proceed as planned.

A mourner viewing the body of Dr. Martin Luther King Jr.
MEMPHIS, TENNESSEE, APRIL 1968 © 1998 BURKE UZZLE

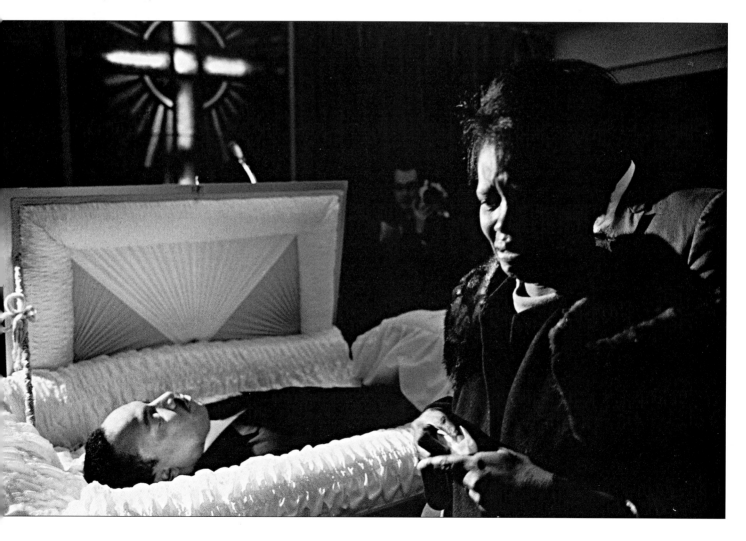

(*Left to right*): Rev. James Bevel, Rev. Jesse Jackson, Rev. Ralph David Abernathy, and Coretta Scott King, key leaders of the SCLC, after Dr. King's assassination

<small>MEMPHIS, TENNESSEE, APRIL 1968 © 1998 BURKE UZZLE</small>

The plane carrying the body of Dr. Martin Luther King Jr. departing for Atlanta, Georgia

<small>MEMPHIS, TENNESSEE, APRIL 1968 © 1998 BURKE UZZLE</small>

Rev. Walter Fauntroy and a Native American woman at a U.S. Congressional hearing on Capitol Hill

WASHINGTON, D.C., LATE APRIL 1968

At the table are Rev. Walter Fauntroy (left) and Rev. Ralph David Abernathy (center) being advised by Marian Wright Edelman at a U.S. Congressional hearing on Capitol Hill.

WASHINGTON, D.C., LATE APRIL 1968

ON APRIL 29, 1968, the Washington phase of the Poor People's Campaign was officially launched with lobbying and media events. Key campaign leaders then dispersed around the country for the formal start-ups of the various caravans that would be coming to Washington—from the West, the South, and the North. My own direct involvement had begun a couple of weeks earlier when I attended a meeting at the Southeast Catholic Center where the SCLC sought volunteers to meet the campaign's communications and public relations needs.

Rev. Ralph David Abernathy with his wife Juanita and a representative group of participants—Native American, African American, Hispanic, and White—at a press conference on Capitol Hill as part of the start of Poor People's Campaign lobbying efforts

WASHINGTON, D.C., LATE APRIL 1968

The Southeast Catholic Center was the site of the initial meeting in April 1968 for those who would become the public relations arm of the Poor People's Campaign.

WASHINGTON, D.C., JUNE 1968

SCLC LEADERS who had been in D.C. left at the end of April to participate in the regional start-ups of the Poor People's Campaign. One group went to Memphis for the start of the southern caravan. This included a march, a demonstration, and the unveiling of the Lorraine Motel plaque marking Dr. King's life and assassination. The Memphis participants and southern caravan organizers then continued to Marks, Mississippi, by car and bus.

Dr. King's brother, A. D. King (in overalls), Rev. Ralph David Abernathy (third from the right), Juanita, his wife, and Rev. Andrew Young (on the end) among the front line leading the kickoff march for the southern caravan of the Poor People's Campaign

MEMPHIS, TENNESSEE, MAY 2, 1968 © 1998 DENNIS BRACK

Buses departing for Marks, Mississippi, the southern caravan's first stop on its way to Washington, D.C.

MEMPHIS, TENNESSEE, MAY 2, 1968

Coretta Scott King, the keynote speaker, at the Mason Temple rally kicking off the southern caravan of the Poor People's Campaign

MEMPHIS, TENNESSEE, MAY 1, 1968

Coretta Scott King and Rev. Ralph David Abernathy dedicating a marble plaque in front of room 306 at the Lorraine Motel, where Dr. King was murdered

MEMPHIS, TENNESSEE, MAY 2, 1968 © 1998 DENNIS BRACK

MRS. CORETTA KING stood on the motel balcony [in Memphis] and told the crowd: "My husband has not been killed. His words speak louder today than ever before to those who cherish his legacy of dignity, nonviolence and love, justice, peace and truth. I dream of the day where not some but all of God's children have food, where not some but all of God's children have decent housing, where not some but all of God's children have a guaranteed annual income in keeping with the principles of liberty and justice."

Memphis Press-Scimitar, May 2, 1968

High school students attending
a freedom rally

MARKS, MISSISSIPPI, EARLY MAY 1968

A couple preparing to board the southern
caravan buses

MARKS, MISSISSIPPI, EARLY MAY 1968

IN EARLY MAY, Rev. James Bevel and others came to Marks from Memphis to organize the continuation of the southern caravan across the South to Washington, D.C. They pitched large tents in a small industrial park just south of town to serve as temporary lodging for the many people—men, women, and families—who were volunteering. Organizing the Mule Train presented a range of social, educational, and logistical challenges, and required ongoing problem solving and replanning by those in charge.

Myrtle Brown at a freedom rally
MARKS, MISSISSIPPI, EARLY MAY 1968

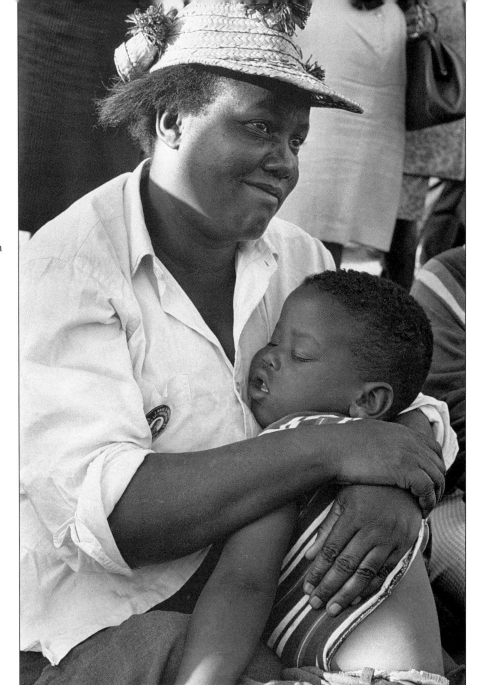

Mother and son at a
freedom rally

MARKS, MISSISSIPPI,
EARLY MAY 1968

People line up to board the southern
caravan buses

MARKS, MISSISSIPPI, EARLY MAY 1968

Standing in the center is SCLS's Rev. James Bevel at a freedom rally organizing for the southern caravan.

MARKS, MISSISSIPPI, EARLY MAY 1968

People preparing to board the southern caravan buses

MARKS, MISSISSIPPI, EARLY MAY 1968

The children of Bertha Johnson: (back row) Brian, Terence, and Nelson; (front row) Trudy, Charles Jr., and Brenda Marie at the Mule Train preparation site

Marks, Mississippi, early May 1968

Men preparing to board the southern caravan buses

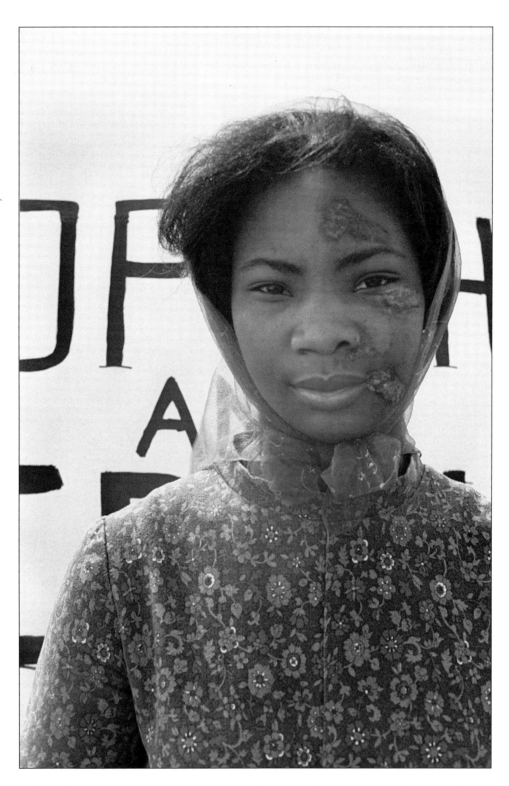

Lydia McKinnon, a schoolteacher who was attacked by police using their rifle butts to disperse people protesting the arrest of Willie Bolden, SCLC organizer and Mule Train Wagon Master

MARKS, MISSISSIPPI, EARLY MAY 1968

THE ORGANIZING EFFORT was complicated by a series of confrontations that included the arrest of the SCLC organizer and Mule Train Wagon Master Willie Bolden, and the beating of several participants in a subsequent protest march. One of those beaten was Lydia McKinnon, then a schoolteacher in Marks, Mississippi. She later said:

> I don't know what came over me. I don't think that I was courageous; it's just that for those few short moments, my life flashed before me. I had been in the segregated South all my life. White folks had the best of everything, and what we blacks were getting was worse than second best, and we were expected to do a good job with hardly anything. So, for that one crazy moment, I stood up for what I knew to be right, and with the butts of their guns and the heels of their boots, they knocked me unconscious for it. My parents asked me: "What got into you–don't you know you could have been killed?" Today, looking back on in it, I probably would not have done what I did; but as that young woman, I was just tired of the way we were being treated.

Local police officers and state troopers look on as people prepare to leave on the southern caravan.

MARKS, MISSISSIPPI, EARLY MAY 1968

Young people waiting to leave on the Mule Train

MARKS, MISSISSIPPI, EARLY MAY 1968

"WHAT WE GET FOR CHOPPING COTTON, you don't make nothing," he said. "People don't want to pay you over $2.50 a day. Sometimes you might make $3." Recently he left the cotton fields for a job in a mill where, he said, he earned $1.25 an hour. "But that job didn't last long," he said. "I got laid off." A week ago, he was called for his physical examination for the Army. "What am I going to do?" he said, repeating the question. "What can you do? If don't nothing happen, the Army or anything like that, I'm going to Washington."

Harry Smiley, quoted in *New York Times*, May 7, 1968

(*Left to right*) Mr. Taper, James Kershaw, and Eddie Keys at the Mule Train preparation site

MARKS, MISSISSIPPI, EARLY MAY 1968

Mules and wagon at the Mule Train preparation site

MARKS, MISSISSIPPI, EARLY MAY 1968

Men and wagon at the Mule Train preparation site

MARKS, MISSISSIPPI, EARLY MAY 1968 © 1998 ERNEST C. WITHERS

MR. BOLDEN also said that the mule train would leave Marks "at noon tomorrow." He said 16 wagons were ready to roll and all but five of the mules had been shod. Shoes will be put onto those five on the road, he said. The mule train has been beset by all kinds of trouble—lack of skilled blacksmiths and wagoneers, few tools, long distances to go for equipment, poor weather and mules stubbornly resisting the idea of shoes.

New York Times, May 13, 1968

Putting shoes on the mules while enroute
MISSISSIPPI, MID-MAY 1968

(below left) Watering the mules on the way to Washington
MISSISSIPPI, MID-MAY 1968

(below right) Two of the mules from the Mule Train
KILMICHAEL, MISSISSIPPI, MAY 22, 1968

Black and white mules at the Mule Train preparation site

Marks, Mississippi, early May 1968

AFTER OVERCOMING the difficulties of equipment, organizing, and what seemed a continuous downpour of Delta rain, the Mule Train set off from Marks on Monday, May 13, 1968, at 3:30 P.M.—about 10 days later than initially scheduled.

(right and below)
The Mule Train gets underway

MARKS, MISSISSIPPI,
MAY 13, 1968

FOR THE FIRST PART of its journey, from Marks, Mississippi, to Birmingham, Alabama, about 115 people—roughly 100 poor people and 15 SCLC–provided staff—traveled with the Mule Train in its fifteen to twenty wagons. Thirty or more people helped to drive the wagons, and another 15 or so served as volunteer staff. There were more than 40 women and almost 20 preteenagers. Ages ranged from 8 months to over 70 years, with more than half being between 17 and 30 years old. The participant roster kept changing as, all along the journey to Washington, new people would join and others would drop out. Two cars and two trucks accompanied us. One truck carried portable toilets and feed for the mules; the second truck carried personal belongings and food for the participants.

Onlookers watching as friends and family pass by on the Mule Train
MARKS, MISSISSIPPI, MAY 13, 1968

The Mule Train gets underway.

Marks, Mississippi, May 13, 1968

The truck carrying portable
toilets accompanies the Mule
Train at a rest stop.

Mississippi, mid-May 1968

Leo Walker weeds his cotton as the Mule Train passes by.

Marks, Mississippi, May 13, 1968

ALL IN ALL, the Mule Train traveled close to five hundred miles in a month. It averaged about twenty-five miles each of the days it was actually on the road, and spent the remainder of the time at rest stops, repairing wagons and attending to other logistics. Travel was not easy: there were the physical rigors of the journey and the threat of confrontations with hostile whites and legal authorities. Daily feeding and sheltering of both passengers and animals were complicated and required a lot of scurrying around and advance arrangements. Despite the intense planning, the preparation of its passengers, and the careful ongoing attention to logistics, the Mule Train faced adversity and challenge as it moved across the country.

(above and below) Mule Train rest stop on the second day out

Batesville, Mississippi, May 14, 1968.

Nick Gable and Myrna Copeland, Mule Train participants

NEAR BATESVILLE, MISSISSIPPI, MAY 14, 1968

A church rally during the Mule Train's journey

MISSISSIPPI, MID-MAY 1968

Rev. Andrew Young,
then a senior member
of the SCLC staff who
helped organize the
Mule Train

Marks, Mississippi,
early May 1968

AS ANDY YOUNG SAYS, the Movement is a movement, and a movement
shouldn't be forced or expected to meet deadlines. A movement of people is
just an upsurge of their opinion and feelings. When you're working with the
feelings of people, you can't be expected to meet deadlines and have
everything go on schedule.

Myrna Copeland

Wagon Master Willie Bolden giving one of his daily pep talks

Marks, Mississippi, early May 1968

ONE OF OUR BIGGEST HEADACHES was that the weather wasn't good. We used to just sit down late in the evening and talk about what life must have been like for the pioneers going out West and how they traveled in mule trains and similar situations. I mean, I know that for us it was raining and cold, and in almost every town that we went into, we didn't sleep in hotels. Some people slept on the wagons, some slept in homes, and others slept in churches. Some people stayed up all night and didn't sleep at all. Most of the time, I took catnaps. I felt responsible for seeing that everybody got a place to sleep, but it was tough.

Willie Bolden

Joan Cashin (1936-1997) volunteered to help organize and prepare the Mule Train.

MARKS, MISSISSIPPI, EARLY MAY 1968

I GAINED THE COURAGE to speak up for myself. I got married young, you see—you understand what I mean? SCLC taught me that there is no harm in speaking up. That's the only way you can let people know what you think and feel.

Bertha Johnson Luster

Mule Train girls playing Ride-Sally-Ride
DUCK HILL, MISSISSIPPI, MAY 20, 1968

At a Mule Train rest stop

Bertha Johnson Luster (right) and friend on the Mule Train

The Mule Train on a gravel road

MISSISSIPPI, MID-MAY 1968

The Mule Train leaving a rest stop
MISSISSIPPI, MID-MAY 1968

THE MULE TRAIN was slowed down because the mules were unaccustomed to highways, paved roads, and shoes, and the wagons were in frequent need of repair. In addition to these and similar complications inherent to the trip, there were several incidents with a significant potential for violence; fortunately, no major injuries or loss of life occurred.

Rev. L. C. Coleman with his banner

GRENADA, MISSISSIPPI, MAY 17, 1968

Mule Train stopped by authorities

EUPORA, MISSISSIPPI, MAY 23, 1968

Toppled Mule Train wagon after being startled by a loud horn on the highway

NEAR COLUMBUS, MISSISSIPPI, MAY 25, 1968

(above and below) Well-wishers greeting the Mule Train, a familiar scene all along the journey

Mississippi State University students wishing the Mule Train well

MISSISSIPPI, MID-MAY 1968

THE MULE TRAIN attracted attention wherever it went. Though the entire experience turned out to be far more of a challenge than initially anticipated, the Mule Train people more than rose to the occasion, and supporters and well-wishers turned out all along the route. As Wagon Master Bolden said:

I think that it was because of unity and commitment, and that we got folks to understand that this was not going to be an easy journey. It had never been done before. We didn't know of anyone in our time that had undertaken such a task. We were going to have to stick together. In the morning, I would give pep talks, and I would preach in the evenings at mass rallies. I would solicit help from the local communities at these meetings. We were received well in almost every community that we stopped in. They were poor folks just like us.

(*Left to right*) Shirley Collins, Jessie Franklin, and Ida Mae Lloyd on a Mule Train wagon

MISSISSIPPI, MID-MAY 1968

Rev. Hosea Williams
speaking at an evening rally
enroute

GRENADA, MISSISSIPPI, MAY 17, 1968

Onlookers along the
Mule Train route

ALABAMA, EARLY JUNE 1968

Dobbie Ann Johnson, held by Jack Franklin

EACH EVENING, when the Mule Train would stop for the day, activity would be in full swing. Food would be inventoried, distributed, and prepared; mules would be watered and fed; wagons and equipment would be inspected and repaired; passengers would access their personal belongings; children would play; and staff would organize rallies, prayer meetings, and community support. All in all, it was an awesome amount of daily logistics to attend to more than a hundred people and their travel across the South.

Watering the mules on the way to Washington
REFORM, ALABAMA, MAY 26, 1968

Children eating at a Mule Train rest stop
NEAR COTTONDALE, ALABAMA, MAY 30, 1968

ON MAY 26, 1968, the Mule Train entered Alabama, having crossed its first of several state lines. As difficult as it had been, there were celebration and relief at having made it through Mississippi virtually without incident.

Bertha Johnson Luster (center) Margorie Hyatt (right) taking inventory of the Mule Train food provisions
Columbus, Mississippi, May 25, 1968

(below) Mississippi state police at the Mississippi-Alabama border
East of Columbus, Mississippi, May 26, 1968

The Mule Train entering Alabama

REFORM, ALABAMA, MAY 26, 1968

THE MULE TRAIN took about two weeks to go through Alabama. Included on its route were its first larger cities: Tuscaloosa and Birmingham. People's curiosity and support were clearly felt, and the seeming incongruity of the Mule Train in the city soon gave way to the obvious parallels we saw between urban and rural poverty.

Wagon Master Willie Bolden conferring with Tuscaloosa police

TUSCALOOSA, ALABAMA, MAY 28, 1968

*(below)*Wagon Master Willie Bolden leading the Mule Train into Tuscaloosa

TUSCALOOSA, ALABAMA, MAY 28, 1968

The Mule Train passing the hotel owned by African-American businessman A. G. Gaston

Birmingham, Alabama, early June 1968

City workers pause as the Mule Train passes

Alabama, early June 1968

ONE OF THE Mule Train's last confrontations with state authorities occurred between Douglasville and Atlanta after Governor Lester Maddox ordered the state police to block its access to an interstate highway: Georgia state troopers halted the mule train segment of the Poor People's Campaign today and arrested 67 persons for trying to take wagons onto busy Interstate 20, but authorities later dropped the charges and opened the highway to the demonstrators. Under the agreement worked out during a 90-minute meeting between Sheriff Caude Abercrombie and wagonmaster Willie Bolden, the mule train will be allowed to travel along the emergency lane of Interstate 20 between the hours of 7 A.M. and 7 P.M. Saturday. Bolden told his 130 demonstrators to spend the night at the Zion Hill Baptist Church and be prepared to move out early Saturday.

June 15, 1968, UPI article in the *Washington Post*

Georgia state troopers lead the Mule Train off the ramp leading to the interstate
Douglasville, Georgia, June 14, 1968 © 1998 UPI/CORBIS-BETTMANN

Mule Train participants kneel and pray after they are stopped from entering Interstate 20

THE MULE TRAIN was far behind schedule when it reached Atlanta. In Washington, many of the key events in the Poor People's Campaign had already occurred and others were imminent—particularly Solidarity Day on June 19. Because the SCLC organizers were eager to have the Mule Train in Washington for what they saw as the culminating rally of the campaign, they decided to send it—participants, mules, wagons, and equipment—by train from Atlanta. On June 17, the participants boarded the train and traveled overnight, arriving in Alexandria the next morning.

(above and facing page) Mule Train paticipants arrive on the train from Atlanta

ALEXANDRIA, VIRGINIA, JUNE 18, 1968

Mrs. Williams arrives on the train from Atlanta
ALEXANDRIA, VIRGINIA, JUNE 18, 1968

(*below*) The Mule Train people boarding a bus at
the train depot
ALEXANDRIA, VIRGINIA, JUNE 18, 1968

A temporary corral for the Mule Train mules

Lee Dora Collins and her daughter
arrive on the train from Atlanta

ALEXANDRIA, VIRGINIA, JUNE 18, 1968

FROM ALEXANDRIA, the Mule Train participants were dispersed throughout the area. Most of them stayed at a Methodist center outside the city, some joined family members or friends who were already at Resurrection City, and others stayed with local families. Based on location, they were bused daily to participate in the various Poor People's Campaign activities.

Andrew Marrsett and Virginia state authorities discussing how to route the Mule Train into Washington
ALEXANDRIA, VIRGINIA, JUNE 19, 1968

People gathered to watch the reassembling of the Mule train

Alexandria, Virginia, June 19, 1968

Reassembling a wagon for the Mule Train's entrance into Washington, D.C.

Alexandria, Virginia, June 19, 1968

The Mule Train on the George Washington Memorial Parkway

Police escorting the Mule Train

Alexandria, Virginia, June 19, 1968 © 1998 Ken Heinen

ON JUNE 19, the Mule Train marchers regathered, reassembled the wagons, and rehitched the mules; the caravan proceeded to the banks of the Potomac River just across from Resurrection City and the Washington Monument.

The Mule Train on the George Washington Memorial Parkway

Arlington, Virginia, June 19, 1968 © 1998 Ken Heinen

THE POOR PEOPLE'S mule train rumbled to the banks of the Potomac yesterday on the last leg of its trek from Mississippi and prepared to join the "Solidarity Day" march in Washington today. The 13 wagons, some of them canting perilously on rickety frames, traveled north from Alexandria on the George Washington Memorial Parkway to a National Park Service maintenance area near the west end of the Memorial Bridge in Virginia, where the mules were bedded down for the night. The six-mile trip took three hours. Traffic was tied up behind the mule train as Alexandria, Arlington County and Park Police shepherded the group along in the curb lane on the northbound side of the Parkway.

Washington Post, June 19, 1968

One of the Mule Train wagons passing in the shadow of the Capitol

WASHINGTON, D.C., JUNE 19, 1968 STEPHEN NORTHUP ©1998 *WASHINGTON POST*

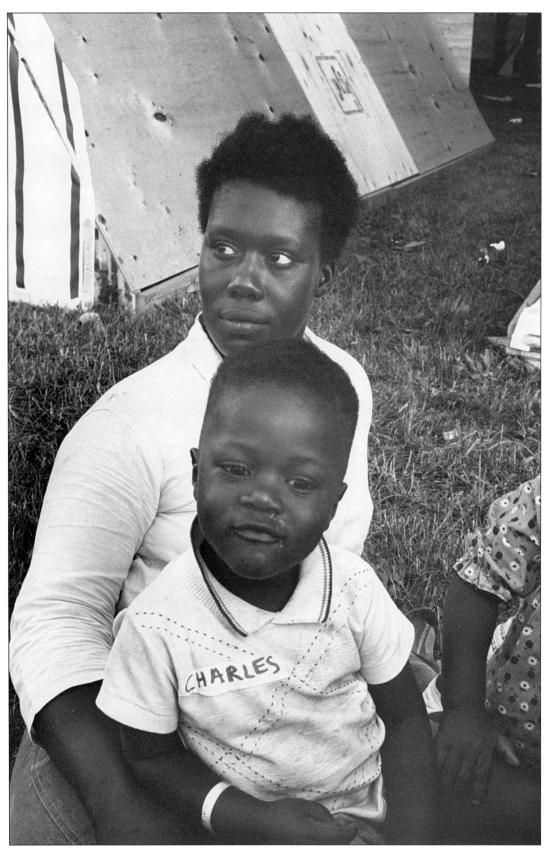

Augusta and Charles Denson in Resurrection City

Washington, D.C., June 1968 © 1998 John Cashin

WITH PERMITS from the National Park Service, a settlement was established on the National Mall along the Reflecting Pool between the Lincoln Memorial and Washington Monument. It was named Resurrection City as a symbol of rebirth from the depths of oppression and hopelessness. Its first residents arrived on May 12, 1968, and it was dedicated the next day. At its peak in June, there were more than seven thousand people in facilities initially anticipated for fifteen hundred to three thousand people.

Resurrection City on the National Mall

WASHINGTON, D.C., MAY 1968 © 1998 ROBERT BURCHETTE—*WASHINGTON POST* STAFF PHOTOGRAPHER

A street of Resurrection City on the National Mall
WASHINGTON, D.C., JUNE 1968

MAY AND JUNE RAINFALLS were far heavier than average, and for much of the time Resurrection City was a veritable quagmire: dirty and slippery, with mud holes one could fall into. With its minimal living conditions, the weather, overcrowding, undercover agents and troublemakers, and conflicts among political and social constituencies, Resurrection City soon became a metaphor for the very conditions being protested by the campaign.

Man washing clothes at Resurrection City
WASHINGTON, D.C., JUNE 1968

Girl in the mud of Resurrection City
WASHINGTON, D.C., JUNE 1968

Some of the more than 50,000 Solidarity Day participants, at the rally along the Reflecting Pool, between the Lincoln Memorial and the Washington Monument

<small>WASHINGTON, D.C., JUNE 19, 1968</small>

A demonstration, part of the Poor People's Campaign

WASHINGTON, D.C., JUNE 1968 © 1998 BERNIE BOSTON

RALLIES, DEMONSTRATIONS, and lobbying continued throughout May and June 1968, and were to culminate in the Solidarity Day Rally for Jobs, Peace, and Freedom. This was scheduled for "Juneteenth," June 19, an important date for African-Americans; it represents the day by which word of Lincoln's Emancipation Proclamation reached slaves in the Deep South. Solidarity Day was a success, with more than fifty thousand people participating in the rally in front of the Lincoln Memorial.

Rev. Ralph David Abernathy (front right) leading a Poor People's Campaign demonstration

Taking part in the Solidarity Day activities are Rev. James Bevel (at the podium), Rev. Jesse Jackson (to the right), O. Thompson (front, far right), and Coretta Scott King (seated with a brooch) and Sen. Edward Brooks (to her left).

WASHINGTON. D.C., JUNE 19, 1968

Standing in the center are three men of the Memphis Sanitation Worker's Union, which Dr. Martin Luther King was supporting at the time of his assassination, taking part in Solidarity Day

WASHINGTON. D.C., JUNE 19, 1968

Solidarity Day participants with signs

Washington, D.C., June 19, 1968

One of the final occupants being forcibly removed from Resurrection City by police

AFTER SOLIDARITY DAY, most campaign participants left for home, but despite the continuing deterioration of conditions in Resurrection City, many also stayed. The campaign's leaders had decided to close down Resurrection City and had arranged with the Department of the Interior to provide a few additional days for an orderly exit on June 25, 1968. Despite this arrangement, the National Guard and local law enforcement units surrounded Resurrection City and removed with force the remaining people. They subsequently leveled the ground.

People being evicted from Resurrection City

Washington, D.C., late June 1968

PART TWO

A Narrative of the Journey

SECTION 1.
THE MULE TRAIN: MARKS TO WASHINGTON

THE ORIGINS AND INITIATION OF THE POOR PEOPLE'S CAMPAIGN

John Hope Franklin and Alfred A. Moss Jr. provide a useful perspective on the social and economic situations being faced by most black people in the South in the postslavery era:

> The cotton crop of 1870 had not reached the level of production achieved just before the war, but by 1880 the South was producing more cotton than ever. While the sugar crop recovered more slowly, its continued improvement was marked. Thus Black farm workers contributed greatly to the economic recovery of the South. As free workers, however, they gained but little. The wages paid them in 1867 were lower than those that had been paid to hired slaves. In the sharecropping system the cost of maintenance was so great that at the end of the year ex-slaves were indebted to their employers for most of what they had made and sometimes more than they had made. The white South generally recovered much more rapidly than the former slaves.[7]

Economically, little had changed by the 1960s: poverty and hunger were rampant; in rural areas, sharecropping was still the rule; jobs were scarce and wages inadequate; and structural and institutional changes were cosmetic at best.

It was in this context that in September 1967, at the SCLC headquarters in Atlanta, Dr. Martin Luther King Jr. met with Marian Wright (later Edelman), an African-American attorney, then the director of the Mississippi office of the NAACP Legal Defense and Education Fund, and four out-of-work African-American men from the Mississippi Delta.[8] These were proud, responsible family men whose unemployment was directly related to lost agriculture, due to ongoing federal government subsidies that rewarded large, wealthy farmers who left land uncropped. This farm policy was especially disastrous to the African-American community in the South and contributed to mass migrations. Unfortunately, the destination cities in the North were ill equipped to provide the jobs, training, and other services required for these migrants to transform their lives; rather, the cycle of poverty most often continued, and the numbers caught in it grew in both the North and the South. To a degree, these four men represented the tip of the iceberg of poverty in America.

Ms. Wright was urging the SCLC to adopt a focus on employment and job training, including among other strategies, demonstrations, sit-ins, and fasts by labor and religious leaders at the Department of Labor offices of then Secretary Willard Wirtz in Washington, D.C. Activities would, continue—with the real possibilities of arrest and jail—until the problems of chronic unemployment and the related plight of the poor were addressed at the national level. Though Dr. King was not convinced of all the particulars, the ideas explored in the meeting became the seeds from which the idea of the Poor People's Campaign grew over the following weeks.

Ms. Wright's core ideas meshed nicely with Dr. King's current thinking about the SCLC and the next steps that should be taken in the Civil Rights movement. He was keenly aware of the importance of broadening its goals and strategies. From difficult and sometimes bitter experiences during prior campaigns, he knew that poverty in all its manifestations needed to be the target, and that the approach would have to encompass all of America's poor. His initial challenge to the nation to reject segregation, and his later speaking out against the war in Vietnam, would be generalized to arouse the conscience of the nation around issues of poverty. Through nonviolent training and mobilization, he hoped to empower poor people in a new movement that transcended race while seeking social and economic justice. Needless to say, these shifts brought with them strategic and organizational complications: old alliances were tested; some were dissolved; new coalitions were required; parochial self-interest would need to be further subsumed; and rhetoric and metaphor would need to be adjusted.

Dr. King announced the Poor People's Campaign in a December 1967 speech, and planning began in early 1968. It was to be the largest and most wide-ranging civil disobedience campaign ever run by the SCLC. Fifteen hundred demonstrators—all well trained in nonviolence—would come to Washington from all around the country, and significant numbers of them would live in temporary housing constructed for that purpose. From that base, the participants would demonstrate and petition the government for an "economic bill of rights." Simultaneously, throughout the country, there would be local demonstrations, organized and led by individuals trained in nonviolent methods. The official SCLC announcement of the Poor People's Campaign came on March 4, 1968, and the SCLC staff fanned out

---

[7] John Hope Franklin and Alfred A. Moss Jr., *From Slavery to Freedom: A History of African Americans* 7th ed. (New York: McGraw-Hill, 1994), 234.

[8] I am indebted to conversations with Ralph Dwan, Marian Wright Edelman, Henry Glassie, Worth Long, Hosea Williams, and Andy Young, among many others, and to Reverend Young's recent book, *An Easy Burden* (especially pp. 437-90), for my understanding of the history of the Poor People's Campaign.

across the country, meeting with and organizing poor Hispanic, Native American, white, and African-American communities for participation.

After a March 18 speech in Memphis, Dr. King, accompanied by Rev. Ralph Abernathy and others, drove to Marks, an impoverished African-American sharecropping community in the Mississippi Delta. As Rev. Abernathy recalled:

> In Marks, Mississippi, I well remember, we visited a day-care center. And Dr. King was moved to tears there. There was one apple, and they took this apple and cut it into four pieces for four hungry waiting students. And when Dr. King saw that, and that is all that they had for lunch, he actually ended up crying. The tears came streaming down his cheek. And he had to leave the room.[9]

Rev. Andrew Young, at that time one of Dr. King's chief lieutenants, remembered the same incident this way:

> We spent time in particular in the impoverished black sharecropping community of Marks, Mississippi. Marks was in the poorest county in the United States, according to the 1960 census. Conditions were so bad Martin actually cried when he saw how people were living. We determined right then and there that the Poor People's Campaign would originate in Marks. A caravan from the Marks community would depart by mule train and be the first to arrive in Washington.[10]

This was to be the first time in almost seventy-five years that anyone had crossed the country by mule-drawn wagons, and it turned out to be far more of a challenge than anyone anticipated. Firsthand experience with mules had become a rarity. American agriculture was mechanized, and mules were used only on a few small farms or kept for nostalgia. So there was a legitimate question as to why they were chosen over horses to bring the poor people to Washington. Mules, the offspring of an ass and a mare, are thought to combine the best of each species. In addition to their greater overall hardiness, stamina, and surefootedness, they are more tolerant than horses of tropical climates.

The following excerpt provides some background on mules in the South:

The South developed a regional culture of "mules and men" which spanned two hundred years. Southerners fervently endorsed the mule in preference to the horse, and defenders of the mule ranged from America's first president to thousands of small farmers throughout the South. The father of our country has also been called the "father" of American mule breeding, for Washington praised the animal and commented on the "great strength of mules, on their longevity, hardiness, and cheap support which gives them preference of horses that is scarcely to be imagined." Washington bred mules on his farm and when he died his will listed fifty-seven mules. Other prominent mule owners in this period included Thomas Jefferson and John Skinner, editor of *American Farmer*. [11]

Southern farmers defended their mules against all other animals and often exaggerated the relative merits of the animal. Their love for the mule was in part a cultural choice and reflected a strong regional sense that "of all animals subservient to agriculture the mule stands preeminent ... he is a long liver, a small consumer, a powerful, faithful and enduring laborer ... superior to the horse in every respect and for every purpose connected with the operations of husbandry." Southern farmers were anxious to have the animals and in 1822 mule colts between eight and ten months of age sold for forty to sixty dollars.

Robert Lamb defines four periods in which mules were widely used throughout the South: (1) the antebellum period (1850-1860); (2) the Civil War and westward expansion to Texas (1860-1900); (3) the mule's ascendancy as the foundation of the southern rural economy (1900-1925); and (4) their decline as tractors were introduced in agriculture (1925-1950).

The SCLC leaders were aware of the important role played by mules in the history of the South and saw them as a valuable metaphor for the economic changes and the resulting impacts on employment on which the Poor People's Campaign would focus. Of the estimated 358,000 mules in Mississippi alone in 1930, only a few remained in 1968. [12]

Dr. Martin Luther King Jr. was assassinated in Memphis on April 4, 1968, in the midst of final

[9] Henry Hampton and Steve Fayer. *Voices of Freedom: An Oral History of the Civil Rights Movement from the 1950s through 1980s* (Blackside Inc., 1990) 456.

[10] Andrew Young, *An Easy Burden* (New York: Harper Collins Publishers, 1996) 450.

[11] Excerpt from "Mules in the South," William R. Ferris, in *Mules and Mississippi*, 1980, Patti Carr Black, editor, the Mississippi Department of Archives and History, Jackson, Mississippi, 5-6.

[12] Cited from *Base Book of Mississippi Agriculture*, Crop and Livestock Reporting Service, Jackson, Mississippi, 1955, in *Mules and Mississippi*, 10.

planning for the Poor People's Campaign. It took the SCLC but a moment to renew its commitment to moving ahead with the campaign, believing firmly that would have been Dr. King's insistence. The Poor People's Committee of one hundred attended to both lobbying and implementation. Athough they were rushed and many details were left unattended that would later come to haunt the campaign, on April 19, Dr. Abernathy formally announced that all would proceed as planned. On April 29, the Washington, D.C., phase of the Poor People's Campaign was officially launched with a couple of days of lobbying and media events. Key campaign leaders then dispersed around the country for the formal start-ups of the various caravans that would be coming to Washington-from the West, the South, and the North. The map on the next page shows the SCLC's initial planning of routes and departure dates.

Undoubtedly, the Poor People's Campaign was changed significantly by Dr. King's death. As his murder became a common source of anger and sorrow across America's ethnic divides, the numbers of groups and individuals intending to participate grew. His death provided a starting point for coalitions and for developing mutual trust and common agendas. However, many of those joining were insufficiently aware of the intended focus and messages of the campaign and untrained in nonviolent methods. As a result, coalitions were sometimes based on inadequate groundwork and activities begun in common often went their separate ways. This had increasingly serious consequences as time went on.

My direct involvement had begun a couple of weeks earlier when I attended an evening meeting at the Southeast Catholic Center, then in the 700 block of Eighth Street, SE, in Washington. Ralph Dwan, who was a priest then (and is now an attorney and legal advocate for the poor in the same Capitol Hill neighborhood), had called the meeting. About twenty-five to thirty people listened as Tom Offenberger, who coordinated communications and public relations for the SCLC, explained the needs of the campaign. About ten folks attended a follow-up meeting a few days later at Mig Boyle-Hoyt's home in Georgetown where we chose our assignments.[13]

I left D.C. at the end of April with those who were going to Memphis for the start of the southern caravan. In Memphis, I participated in the march, demonstration, and unveiling of the Lorraine Motel

plaque marking Dr. King's life and assassination. Then, I traveled with the Memphis participants and southern caravan organizers who went to Marks by car and bus. From there, most continued their journey to Washington in motorized vehicles; those on the Mule Train remained in Marks and completed preparations for their long trip, anticipating eventually reconnecting with those who had gone ahead. The Mule Train had begun its journey of hope.

The following local coverage from Memphis and Marks adds detail to this summary. The first article, "Mrs. King and Abernathy to Speak at Poor People's March Rally Here Tonight," is from the Wednesday, May 1 edition of the *Memphis Press-Scimitar*:

The Poor People's March on Washington, planned by the Southern Christian Leadership Conference, begins in Memphis tomorrow.

A kickoff is planned tonight, with Mrs. Coretta King, widow of Dr. Martin Luther King, to speak at 7:30 at Mason Temple.

Mrs. King and Dr. Ralph Abernathy, King's successor as leader of the SCLC, are to lead the march, starting from the Lorraine Hotel, where Dr. King was shot. The marchers will trek to Marks, Miss., where a "wagon train" will be organized for the march to Washington.

'CONSTRUCTIVE'
In Washington, Dr. Abernathy told cabinet leaders the march will yield "constructive results" in persuading Congress to act on new job, housing and anti-poverty programs.

"We intend to dramatize the plight of America's poor of all races and make very clear that they are sick and tired of waiting for a better life," he said.

OUTLAYS
Abernathy and a committee of 100, representing poor whites, Indians, Puerto Ricans and Mexican-Americans as well as Negroes, have been in Washington since Monday, meeting with Cabinet officers and congressional leaders to urge "massive" government outlays to upgrade the living standards of the poorest Americans.

Nine separate caravans of poor people are scheduled to converge on Washington from south, north, east and west, arriving between May 12 and May 19.

Leaders of the march have no accurate idea at this time how many people will be involved, but they say the number will be in the thousands. They plan to live in a temporary "shanty town" at a still undetermined site in the capital and conduct demonstrations for a period of at least several weeks.

<hr>

[13] I don't have any record of who attended these meetings, but I do remember that Sam Smith and Vince De Forrest were at both. Smith was then the editor of the *D.C. Gazette*, which later became the *Progressive Review*. When I became a photographer, Sam was the first person to hire me, and we've remained good friends since then. He still lives in Washington where he is a writer and political commentator. Vince De Forrest is an African-American Quaker with a continuing commitment to social action.

INTENDED PARTICIPATION IN THE POOR PEOPLE'S CAMPAIGN

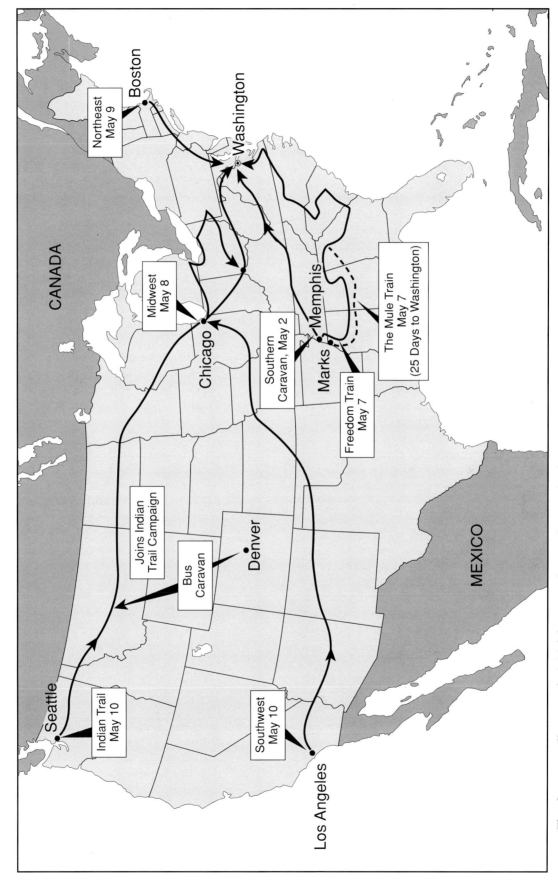

CANADA

MEXICO

Boston
Northeast
May 9

Washington

Midwest
May 8

Chicago

Memphis

Southern
Caravan, May 2

Marks

Freedom Train
May 7

The Mule Train
May 7
(25 Days to Washington)

Joins Indian
Trail Campaign

Bus
Caravan

Denver

Seattle

Indian Trail
May 10

Southwest
May 10

Los Angeles

The above map illustrates the initial departure dates and routes for the caravans coming to Washington, D.C., for the Poor People's Campaign. All of these original departure dates were later revised.

Abernathy said House and Senate leaders with whom he conferred yesterday were "concerned" about possible violence in connection with the demonstrations.

"But we assured them that this will be an entirely peaceful, nonviolent exercise of the people's constitutional right to petition their government for redress of grievances," he said.

Rank and file congressmen continued their angry criticism, however.

Rep. Joel T. Broyhill (R-Va.) said he would continue to try to amend appropriations bills to prevent federal funds from being paid to anyone convicted of rioting, and Rep. Robert Sikes (D-Fla.) demanded that leaders of the march make full financial disclosure to prove "they are not using the poor people for their own purposes."

If leaders of the march were revealed to be "Simon Poor [sic]," Sikes said, "the marchers could have greater confidence in their leaders."

Broyhill, whose anti-riot amendment has already been attached to appropriation bills for the Office of Economic Opportunity (OEO) and the Health, Education and Welfare Department (HEW), said he would ask the House to attach similar riders to money bills for the agriculture department, which administers federal food programs, and all other U.S. agencies.

RECRUITING

At a Clayborn Temple press conference today the Rev. James Bevel, official of the Southern Christian Leadership Conference, said the Memphis contingent leaving at 2 p.m. tomorrow would probably walk to the city limits and then go by vehicle to Marks, Miss., for several days of recruiting.

He said that in Washington the Memphians would build the City of Hope—the shanty town. Enroute to Washington the Marks-Memphis group will make recruiting stops in Nashville, Knoxville and Danville, Va.

In Memphis Mrs. King will have room 306 at the Lorraine Hotel—the room where her husband stayed before he was shot.

The next day, Thursday, May 2, the *Memphis Press-Scimitar* printed "500 Begin 'Poor March' After Rally in Memphis":

Led by a wagon pulled by two old, skinny mules, a crowd of about 500 marchers singing civil rights songs moved down Memphis streets on the first leg of the "Poor People's March" today.

Some wore still new overalls and straw hats, some were in sport clothes, but most carried suitcases or knapsacks as they marched under the hot, May sun.

From the Lorraine Hotel, where memorial services were held below the balcony where the late Dr. Martin Luther King Jr. was slain, the marchers moved in orderly fashion to Main and S. Parkway to catch chartered buses for Marks, Miss.

DESTINATION D.C.

From Marks they will go to Washington as part of the campaign for poor people that Dr. King envisioned before his death.

Police walked on either side of the marchers 30 to 40 feet apart and patrol cars and police motorcycles moved with the crowd. Traffic police blocked off the intersections as the marchers came to them.

Before the march began, a cheering, chanting crowd of about 1,000 gathered below the balcony for the memorial services.

Mrs. Coretta King stood on the motel balcony and told the crowd:

"My husband has not been killed. His words speak louder today than ever before to those who cherish his legacy of dignity, nonviolence and love, justice, peace and truth.

"I dream of the day where not some but all of God's children have food…where not some but all of God's children have decent housing…where not some but all of God's children have a guaranteed annual income in keeping with the principles of liberty and justice."

As Rev. Ralph Abernathy, successor to Dr. King as head of the Southern Christian Leadership Conference, came out on the balcony, the crowd cheered him and chanted: "Who shall lead us? Abernathy."

THEY SING

Abernathy led the crowd in singing "Rock of Ages," one of King's favorite hymns, and a "litany of remembrance" to Dr. King. Abernathy wore blue denim overalls with a blue denim coat.

Abernathy announced that Dr. King's brother, Rev. A. B. King of Louisville, Ky., a long-time member of the SCLC board of directors, had joined the SCLC staff.

Abernathy told the crowd: "We don't have any hate in our hearts for Memphis because it was ordained that Dr. King was going to die and he did. He could have died in Nashville or anywhere. It was his time. But the people of Memphis feel they ought to do something."

In the crowd were O. W. Pickett, a real estate man, Gerald Fanion, deputy director for the Tennessee Council of Human Relations, and Mrs.

Cornelia Crenshaw, longtime Memphis Housing Authority employee working to unionize MHA workers, all in new overalls.

A large marble slab to be mounted at the motel near where Dr. King was shot was carried out during the service. The slab has temporary lettering painted on it now but the words are to be carved later, with a Biblical quotation.

FREED ON BOND

Seven advance organizers of the Southern Christian Leadership Conference, arrested in Marks yesterday, were released on bond today.

The seven were jailed after attempting to recruit Negro high school pupils.

Their leader, Willie Bolden, accused Mississippi highway patrolmen of brutality and accused L. C. Price, a Negro and one of the three Marks policemen, of "helping them."

Price pushed his way through the crowd to face Bolden and said: "You're a damned liar." Bolden turned away from him.

IN SUPPORT

About 175 persons marched on the Marks courthouse this morning in support of the seven organizers. Two dozen unarmed highway patrolmen watched the proceedings at the courthouse, but when Bolden began denouncing them, they walked to their cars, put on their helmets and picked up unloaded shotguns.

Bolden was arrested after the high school principal called in officers to stop recruiting, complaining that the "school was in an uproar." A group of 350 students from the school started a sit-in on the lawn of Quitman County jail to protest Bolden's arrest.

FLYING WEDGE

The sit-in was broken up by about 20 highway patrolmen who moved into the group in a flying wedge, carrying rifles and shotguns.

Sheriff L. V. Harrison said no one was seriously hurt. "All was quiet last night and this morning," he said. "They had a little march of about 250 people last night, from Third Street to the Courthouse and back." (The march began at the Marks home Dr. King had chosen for his headquarters when he envisioned the start of the "Poor People's Campaign" in the town.)

MARCH PLANS

The last plans for the caravan to Marks were announced last night at a mass rally in memory of Dr. King at Mason Temple 938 Memphis, attended by Mrs. King and Abernathy.

During the rally at Mason Temple last night,

Abernathy told over 9,000 persons: "Any of you wish to tarry around the cemetery and moan around the grave of Martin Luther King, I've got news for you. We've got business on the road."

'NONVIOLENT'

"Nothing would please the power structure more than if we stopped simply because they killed our leader," he said. "We're going back to Washington with thousands of poor people to stay until Congress does something for us. This is going to be a nonviolent campaign."

Abernathy said the march will represent all segments of the poor, including whites from the Appalachia area, Indians, Mexican-Americans and Puerto Ricans.

"Under Dr. King's leadership, we were going to reel and rock and shake America until everything fell into place," he said. But under his own leadership, "we're going to turn it upside down," he said.

HIS REPLY

After Abernathy gave his prepared speech, he said he had been asked why the march wasn't held at a later date when the climate would be better. He said he replied:

"The black man has waited for 350 years and he will wait no more. We are not asking for our rights, we are demanding them. No longer will we scratch our heads for Mr. Charley."

Earlier, Mrs. King told the audience she believes a great transformation is taking place in the world.

"We need this thing for, as my husband used to say, if you save the soul of America, the rest of the world will have a chance," she said.

SINGS SPIRITUAL

A former concert singer, Mrs. King then sang the Negro spiritual, "Sweet Little Jesus Boy," which was a favorite of her husband's.

Mrs. King was met by eight detectives and two patrolmen on her arrival at Memphis Metropolitan Airport yesterday. She had originally planned to stay in the room her husband had at the Lorraine Motel but instead she stayed in Room 207. She was expected to return to Atlanta after the memorial service today.

The Memphis marchers are to board a "freedom train," probably Sunday, at Clarksdale, Miss., and go to Washington to build a shantytown for the "Poor People's Campaign." The shantytown is to be called "The City of Hope."[14]

14 The temporary community on the Mall wound up being called Resurrection City. According to Reverend Young, "City of Hope" turned out to be the name of an existing charity which objected to its use. Young, *An Easy Burden*, 481.

WAGON TRAIN

Abernathy Tuesday will start a wagon train on its way to the nation's capital through Mississippi, Alabama and Georgia.

Rallies in Chicago, Boston and Denver next week are to start other portions of the campaign.

Rev. James Bevel, SCLC official, said the Memphians would build a shanty city in Washington and return in 10 to 14 days "so that the students can take their final exams."

Harry Sharp, director of attendance for city schools, said the decision whether to readmit students who join the march would have to be made by the elected members of the Memphis Board of Education, and not the staff.

PROCEDURE

If students leave school they are usually suspended and must discuss their readmittance with staff members.

"But this would have to be a board decision," he said. "This centers around a particular thing…it is not a normal situation.

"We would want the full backing of the board before making any decision."

Bevel was asked about the mule-pulled wagon that was to be used in one part of the march. He said the SCLC has obtained 10 to 12 mules but is having a hard time locating more. "We need a lot more but mules aren't used in farming any more," he said. "I guess South America is about the only place we could find all the mules we need."

The same day, Thursday, May 2, the *Memphis Press-Scimitar* printed a related editorial, "Abernathy and the March":

The Rev. Ralph Abernathy and the small vanguard of the poor people's campaign organized by the late Dr. Martin Luther King Jr. wound up winners in their three days of meeting with Washington officialdom.

It's too bad they can't quit while they are ahead. But the long-planned march to Washington by several thousand needy persons already is under way, and Abernathy, successor to Dr. King as head of the Southern Christian Leadership Conference, seems determined that it continue.

After a rally here last night attended by the Rev. Abernathy and Mrs. Coretta King, widow of Dr. King, and a memorial service for Dr. King this morning, a Memphis delegation to the march was scheduled to head for Marks, Miss., staging point for a train trip to Washington.

* * *

In Washington, Abernathy and his advance party were received courteously, even warmly, by most cabinet officers and congressional leaders to whom they addressed their demands. Even those officials kept waiting for hours and tongue-lashed—sometimes for problems over which they had no jurisdiction—responded civilly to their tardy visitors.

Many of their listeners readily endorsed the goals of more meaningful jobs, better housing, more liberal welfare benefits, more food for the hungry, and federal programs more responsive to need. In fact it would be a mean-spirited fellow who could not agree to these aims.

But the problem is not lack of compassion but of resources—both human and financial—to cure all of a sudden the accumulated ills of centuries. Already government is spending more and working harder to root out poverty and its complex causes than ever in our history. And the visit of Abernathy and his vanguard amply made the case for even greater effort.

The main body of marchers of course, has every right to march and petition, as the administration has made clear. But some of their leaders have threatened "militant" civil disobedience if Congress doesn't snap to—a technique unlikely to win congressional sympathy. Nor can the possibility that the lawless will use the march to forment [sic] violence be dismissed. This would further deplete the existing fund of goodwill in Washington.

If the marchers must march, they would best serve their cause by making their Washington visit as brief, constructive and orderly as possible.

Another Memphis paper, *Commercial Appeal*, printed in their Friday, May 3 edition this article by Larry Scroggs, "Emotion Outpaces Mules As Poor People's March Steps Off From Fatal Spot":

Dr. Martin Luther King Jr.'s Poor People's March yesterday moved out at a mule's pace from the spot where he was felled by an assassin's bullet April 4.

A symbolic, two-and-three-quarter mile march from the Lorraine Motel through Memphis slum areas was brisk and orderly and marked by spirituals sung by a group of marchers police estimated at 400 to 500.

The last of eight chartered Greyhound Scenicruisers [sic] roared away from Michigan and South Parkway East at 3:50 p.m., carrying about 350 people on their way to Marks. Miss., the first stop on the way to Washington.

An hour and 20 minutes later, the buses discharged their passengers at the small clapboard Zion AME Church on Highway 3, in the heart of the Negro district in Marks.

A lack of lights and water at the tent campgrounds sent some of the marchers back to Memphis last night after a peaceful march around the Marks town square. Most of the others bowed to the darkness and mosquitoes and spent the night at churches and private homes.

The Rev. Ralph Abernathy, march leader, was to leave Marks about 2 a.m. today to organize another march from the Jackson, Miss., area.

Seven advance organizers were taken into custody in Marks Wednesday during a clash with police that stemmed from efforts to recruit high school students.

All seven were freed on bond earlier yesterday, but town officials were still apprehensive.

About 20 Mississippi Highway Patrol cars prowled the streets of the town of 2,700 people, where the median income is $1,517.

At the end of an hour and a half memorial service at the motel, Dr. King's successor as SCLC president, the Rev. Mr. Abernathy, dramatically signaled the beginning of the march by saying, "The moment has come. The day of weeping has ended: the day of march has begun."

The strains of "We Shall Overcome" swelled in the amphitheater-like area under the balcony of the Lorraine Motel.

Arms interlocked, a crowd of nearly 1,000 swayed as they hummed the tune while the Rev. Mr. Abernathy implored, "If you cannot go all the way to Marks, you can go part of the way—where the buses are waiting."

Moments before, about 12:30 p.m., Dr. King's widow, Mrs. Coretta King, led those gathered in memory of her husband in the familiar hymn said to be his favorite—"Softly And Tenderly."

Mrs. King's clear voice soared above the crowd.

Earlier, she stood at the spot where her husband fell and said, "On this spot where my husband gave his life, I pledge my eternal loyalty and devotion to the work he so nobly began."

A gray marble tablet, inscribed with a cross and a gold star, was unveiled. It read, "Martin Luther King Jr., Jan. 15, 1929-April 4, 1968. Founding President of the Southern Christian Leadership Conference."

It contained a quote from Genesis, Chapter 37, "They said to one another, 'Behold, here cometh the dreamer... Let us slay him... And we shall see what will become of his dreams.'"

The plaque will be installed in the window of the room in which Dr. King spent his last night.

The march through Memphis' streets took an hour and 20 minutes. A rickety farm wagon, pulled by mules named Ada and Bully, led the march.

The Rev. Mr. Abernathy and Dr. King's brother, the Rev. A. D. King, took the reins at the halfway point on the route and drove the rest of the way.

When the march turned onto Texas Street, the heart of the Memphis slum area, the Rev. Mr. Abernathy ordered a halt.

Three times he left the main group and climbed worn steps of the rundown buildings to greet residents. He told Mrs. Olivia Wright, 68, of 1209 Texas and her daughter, Mrs. Wilma Spiller, 35, who is almost blind, that he was going to Washington to help remedy their plight.

The two women live in a $25 a month, two-story structure and said they "wanted to go to church but didn't have any clothes they could wear."

"Here are two of our sisters," the SCLC president shouted to the crowd. "They're living here with these rats and roaches and all they have is a little welfare and Social Security money."

All along the route residents waved from their porches and street corners as they watched the marchers go by. Many waved back and some shouted, "We're going to do something about the way you have to live."

Two Negro patrolmen, T. Miller and R. E. Confer, preceded the mule-drawn wagon owned by Mack Woods, 73, of 381½ North Main. They were the only officers among the marchers, although a large number of others were stationed at intersections along the way.

On Friday, May 3, the Memphis *Commercial Appeal* covered the situation in the article "Marks 'Stopover' May Be Longer," by Gregory Jaynes:

Marks, Miss., May 2—More than 1,000 marchers tramped around the antebellum courthouse here twice Thursday night, listened to the Rev. Ralph Abernathy threaten to stay in Marks until "we straighten things out," and then walked to an industrial park on the edge of town to bed down for the night.

The Poor People's March on Washington had run through its first day, but a lack of facilities caused many of the marchers to scatter last night.

The crowd, about 300 of whom had ridden to Marks from Memphis earlier in the day, assembled in front of the courthouse and heard the Rev. Mr. Abernathy ask for a bullhorn from the Mississippi State Highway Patrolmen sitting in about 25 cars parked in the area. There was no response.

Without the bullhorn, the Rev. Mr. Abernathy said:

"We're sticking together. Arrest one of us, you'll have to arrest all of us. I understand the mayor here hasn't lived up to his promise. There's no water for us where we'll be camping tonight, no lights and no toilets. Marks was just a stop on the way to Washington. We'll have to stay until we straighten things out."

Small, heavily-tanned Howard Langford, mayor of Marks, said he's been ready to meet demands for water every since march organizers got here, but "they've changed their mind four times about a campsite in the last two days.

"Do you know when I found out where they were actually going to camp? At 3 o'clock this afternoon."

The former theater operator said he's had crews ready for two days to run water to the campsite. About lights, he said that was the power company's problem, not the city's.

"They brought their own food and trucks," he said—mistakenly.

But he maintained the calm and cooperative posture which has "shocked" at least one Southern Christian Leadership Conference organizer.

In Marks, the seven organizers arrested yesterday were released without bond.

And Mayor Langford said of the Rev. Mr. Abernathy's threat to stay in Marks: "They can just stay here as long as they want to."

The lack of lights and the mosquitoes which one marcher called "as big as horseflies" caused most of the marchers to seek places other than the tents. Some came back to Memphis while others sought shelter in churches and private homes.

The atmosphere in Marks was a contrast to the nervous chatter on buses arriving at the town of 2,700 which is rated as one of the poorest in the nation (per capita income of $1,517).

"My knees are shaking like hell," said Leonard Saxton. "Look at them blue sticks. There's cops all over the place down here."

"I hope I don't get shot down here," said another passenger.

The crowd spilled out of the buses when they arrived from Memphis at the small Zion AME Church in the heart of the Negro district. The church holds about 150.

Some 350 people got out. More than 70 piled

back in, for the ride back, apparently with changed minds.

Marchers and mule trains are scheduled to leave Marks on Sunday for Clarksdale.

It seemed like a small beginning.

But Gov. Lester Maddox of Georgia yesterday urged the federal government to issue an injunction to stop it. If it doesn't, he said, it is "courting revolution."

He said the campaign is encouraged "by the Communists to bring America to her knees through disorder, division, rioting, looting, injury and death."

But in Marks last night, it was quiet.

■ ■ ■

ORGANIZING THE MULE TRAIN

There was more to organizing the Mule Train than had been anticipated, and the work was complicated by what seemed to be a continuous Delta rain. Ultimately, we departed from Marks on May 13, about ten days later than originally scheduled. The first obstacle to overcome was locating, purchasing, and transporting mules, wagons, and equipment to Marks. The interview with Joan Cashin and Myrna Copeland and the comments by John Cashin provide details of these activities and the final preparations of the wagons.

In early May, I left Memphis with Rev. James Bevel and others involved in organizing the southern caravan and accompanied them to Marks. They pitched large tents in a small industrial park just south of town to serve as temporary lodging for the many people—men, women, and families—who were volunteering. These tents were also used for "freedom rallies," a frequent occurrence during the days prior to the caravan's departure for Washington.

Organizing the Mule Train presented a range of social, educational, and logistical challenges, and required ongoing problem solving and replanning by those in charge. The organizing, while quite successful despite the seeming chaos, brought with it a series of confrontations—some violent. The following newspaper articles provide perspectives on the broader context in Marks during the organizing for the Poor People's Campaign, and they shed light on why people wanted to participate.

The first article, "Mississippi Mayor Backs Goals of March of Poor," by Walter Rugaber, is from the Saturday, May 4, 1968 edition of the *New York Times*:

Marks, Miss., May 3—Howard C. Langford, a soft-spoken white man who has served for 18 years as Mayor of this quiet town in the Delta region of northwestern Mississippi, endorsed "the goals but not the methods" of the Poor Peoples' Campaign today.

The Mayor's remarks came after he had met at City Hall with leaders of the predominatly Negro antipoverty project, which began a march to Washington yesterday in Memphis, 70 miles north of here. The demonstrators, after marching through Memphis, came here by bus.

"We need in this area industry that would employ more people, both white and colored," he said. "That's why I endorse their goals. If we can get a lot of industry to put people to work, our problems and the Government's problems will be solved."

SEEK MARCH VOLUNTEERS

His partial endorsement of the crusade, sponsored by the Southern Christian Leadership Conference, was remarkable for an official serving in an area where white supremacy is well established. But it was characteristic of the accommodating posture the town has adopted recently.

The Mayor's policies have placed him under considerable strain. Last night, for example, he was under heavy pressure from white businessmen to declare a curfew. There had been no real trouble, however, and the Mayor refused.

The 62-year-old official, haggard and unshaven, remarked this afternoon that he had gone without rest for several days.

Participants in the Poor Peoples' Campaign decided to stop here because Quitman County, of which Marks is the seat, is one of the nation's poorest. They sought today to recruit new march volunteers here. The marchers, to be joined in Washington by groups from other parts of the country, hope to influence Congress to action.

Mr. Langford and other white leaders wanted to avoid a confrontation with the antipoverty campaign and decided to permit the visitors to erect large circus-type tents on city property.

The marchers chose a 44-acre industrial park just south of town, and this morning Mr. Langford went there personally to supervise the installation of lights, a water line and outdoor toilets.

WANT TOWN TO BE 'NORMAL'

The utilities were installed by city employees, at the city's expense. The Mayor said they would have been available when the marchers arrived yesterday if the site had not been chosen at the last minute. The several hundred marchers spent last night in private homes.

The official approach here presented a striking contrast to past attitudes in this state. Only a few years ago, for example, marchers were teargassed in Canton, Miss., when they tried to erect tents on public property. Women and children were in the group.

City and county officials openly admit their strategy is aimed at denying the demonstrators an issue and getting them out of town as quickly and as smoothly as possible.

"We're trying to get the town to be just as normal as possible," said an official who asked not to be quoted by name. "We try to give these people [the demonstrators] an opportunity to march any time they want to march."

"We aren't mad so much as we are nervous," another white source said. "This is just a little old small town, and it's not equipped to handle something like this. It makes for a tense situation, but there doesn't seem to be any anger here."

The next article, "The 20th Century Tests Marks, Mississippi," by Robert Maynard, is from the Sunday, May 5, 1968 edition of the *Washington Post*:

Marks, Miss., May 4—This little Delta Town, whose rural southern traditions are deep and abiding, has already experienced a minor revolution affecting the Negro community to its very core.

An old woman, who had been sitting on her front porch watching the world drift by on Route 3 for 34 years, tells the story of a town and its racial history in a sentence:

"Those people there across them tracks—they use a Negro for what they want, but they don't respect him, and here on this side, the Negroes done decided they ain't gonna take it no more."

Fear, they say here, has been the companion of every Negro as he walks these dusty streets, past the open drain ditches, on his way to meet the white man for his daily bread.

The talk of Marks, these last few weeks, has been about the Poor People's Campaign and about the need in Marks for "something to change the way things have been there."

"The scared Negro already left for Chicago," a young woman quipped at a rally here the other night. But the real scare has been in the older generation, the people past 40. And the challenge to the system is coming now from the very young.

One sees few Negroes in their 20s and 30s on the streets of Marks. They are the ones who have gone in search of a better life to Chicago and Detroit, New York and Boston.

Mandy Wilkins, who supports her four children by driving to a factory job in Lambert, just south of here, is one of the exceptions. She is 25.

Why did she stay?

"Listening to old people talk," Mrs. Wilkins says, "that's what kept me here."

But there are signs that even the old are changing and those who cannot, leave the rallies and the marches to others.

The Rev. James Bevel, in an appeal actually directed at the young, said here at a mass rally, "Old people, you have been lying to us" by teaching fear and respect of white, simply because they're white. He accused them of having lied so much to the white man that they began believing the lie.

Mr. Bevel, the Southern Conference's ranking organizer here, said:

"They have made a habit of lying to the white man and to themselves. The white man says, 'How are you all doing over there?' And they say, 'Fine, thank you, suh, just fine.' Now they are lying to that man. Things are not fine over here. Things are a mess and it's time to tell that to that white man."

The young roar their approval. They say that they are ready to tell the man the way it really is, and they demand changes, with the help of the SCLC.

But among the older people, too, there is evidence that Mr. Bevel's charge reflects the past more than the present.

Perhaps many are still telling the white man across the Illinois Railroad track that all is well, but they no longer say so among themselves.

J. L. Pride is the first Negro policeman on the 3 man Marks force, but the Negro community is not proud of his appointment.

"Look at him," said a 68-year-old woman as the policeman drove by. "How could the man betray his own people that way."

But it is the economic harshness of Marks' employment system that has contributed most to the changing mood of the city's Negroes.

One woman, whose husband drives 80 miles to Memphis for work, recently quit her job as a maid because, he said, "these people don't want workers. What they want is slaves." She said she was paid $3 for a 12-hour day, or 25 cents an hour.

That is why, the woman said, she and the others are glad that the Poor People's Campaign has come to Marks.

"But you have to understand," another said, "that some people are for it (the Campaign) and can't say they are for it. I don't know as how you can blame a man who has a job. Jobs are scarce in these parts."

There is the generation gap of Marks. There is the difference between the older generation and the children and the SCLC organizers.

It is not that the older people do not favor the Campaign. This community is solidly committed. But the young support it loudly and the old support it in whispers.

The next one, "'Poor People' Prepare To Begin Capital Trek," is an Associated Press story from the Monday, May 6 edition of the *Clarion Ledger* in Jackson, Mississippi:

Marks (AP)—At this early stage of its confused recruiting and organization here in the Mississippi Delta, the Poor People's campaign wouldn't impress Congress much.

Things have not gone smoothly. Even the old second-hand van, once a Health Department's mobile chest X-ray unit, ran out of gas while hauling recruiters around Quitman County.

HAD TO PUSH

The young Negroes, packed inside the van like little fish in a can, had to pile out and push their makeshift bus to a gas station.

"Black Power!" hooted one amused white onlooker.

The four large circus-like tents, erected as temporary living quarters for the 220 Memphis Negroes bussed here Thursday as recruiters, stand almost deserted at night.

Plastic air mattresses were doled out but no blankets arrived. The city-bred youngsters, most of them teen-agers but some as young as 12, preferred to spend the nights at Negro homes.

Southern Christian Leadership Conference leaders shrug off such trifles. The over-all picture of the effort to organize a new political force is bright, they say—perhaps a little too bright.

"Actually, we have laid more groundwork and got more things going than in anything else we have ever done," the Rev. Andrew Young, No. 2 man in the SCLC, said Sunday.

PERHAPS TOO FAST

The rub is not that recruiting may go slowly, Young said, but that it may go entirely too fast.

SCLC's master plan called for caravans of poor—black or white—to converge on Washington from all sections of the nation for demonstrations to back demands for new economic programs aimed at banishing poverty.

"We started with plans for three caravans," said Young. "Now what have we got? something like nine. There may be a lot of people. I would be happier if we showed up in Washington with about 2,000."

The caravans—including a symbolic column

of mule-drawn wagons—would supply the "poor power" for early demonstrations, slated to start about May 20 after the erection of a shanty town in Washington.

But too much "poor power" at the start could pose complications. The bigger the crowd, the more difficult it is to feed, to house—and to control.

To the nonviolent SCLC, maintaining control is a major preoccupation.

RECALL RIOT

SCLC leaders remember Memphis, where a few young militants infiltrated a march led by the late Dr. Martin Luther King Jr. and succeeded in triggering a riot.

The daily demonstrations of "poor power" at the nation's capital will be climaxed by a massive march May 30—which is when the SCLC wants its big, impressive crowd. Young figures the march that day will involve more than 100,000 people.[15]

"We might try to keep 20,000 of them in Washington," he said.

But right now, here in the delta, all this seems improbable and far away. Schedules change frequently. A "mule train" is supposed to carry new recruits for the march on Washington out of here Tuesday—but Young says it may be Thursday or Friday, instead.

The Rev. James Bevel, an SCLC field organizer, said physical examinations have been arranged for some 500 Quitman County Negro volunteers to weed out the unfit.

The Rev. Ralph Abernathy, who became head of the SCLC when Dr. King was assassinated in Memphis April 4, goes from Atlanta to Edwards, Miss., to get a caravan started toward Washington Monday with Selma, Ala., as its first stop.

Another article about volunteering for the campaign, "The Poor People of the South: Why Some Want to Join March to Washington," by Earl Caldwell, appeared in the Tuesday, May 7, 1968 edition of the *New York Times*:

Marks, Miss., May 6—Inside the wooden frame church on Second Street some of them signed the little white cards and then went out into the warm afternoon. Others sat quietly on the scarred benches with their belongings at their feet and waited.

For most of them, it would be their first trip outside the Deep South.

"One reason I want to go," a 19-year-old Harry Smiley explained, "is if all the towns is like this one, we need to go."

Harry Smiley is a thin, very dark Negro. Like most of the others who sat in the crude wooden pews at the Eudora African Methodist Episcopal Church, he had just signed up to go to Washington and join the Poor People's Campaign.

Some of them had come here to Marks from nearby Memphis, Tenn., and they carried their clothing with them. Many did not have suitcases. They carried the few belongings that they would take along in cloth sacks and in paper shopping bags.

JOINED BY DELTA GROUP

Now they were being joined by volunteers from the Mississippi Delta like Harry Smiley. These volunteers had just come to sign up, to let the staff of the Southern Christian Leadership Conference know that they would go along. They did not know the people from Memphis, so most of them just signed the cards and left.

Aside from those who came from Memphis, only the older people waited around. They sat near the back of the church and talked quietly among themselves.

"My daughter is going," one of the women remarked. "She thinks I should go too but I don't have sufficient clothes. I wouldn't just want to go anyway. I don't know though. Before they leave I'll have my mind made up."

Only the young did not hesitate.

"My mother doesn't want me to go," a girl who said she was 19 years old explained. "But I'm going anyhow. I just have to go. I just have to go."

Outside Eudora Church the sidewalk was crowded with dark faces and across the street almost totally ignored, was a string of white police cars with long aerials jutting up from their rear bumpers. Mississippi State highway patrolmen, most of them in dark glasses, leaned against the cars or sat inside them and stared across the narrow, dusty street.

Marks is a small town with a population estimated at 3,000 persons. Just beyond the first major intersection, the Negro section begins, with its decaying slate gray wood houses.

The little church, which is only a few blocks from the intersection that divides the town, reflects the poverty of its congregation. There are only the rows of shabby pews, the lights and the posters.

The lights are spaced evenly above the center aisle, hanging from the ceiling on dull links of metal chain.

'BLACK IS BEAUTIFUL'

On one wall there is a string of red and white posters that bear the inscriptions "Jesus Saves," "God Is Love" and "God Bless Our Home." On

[15] This march was rescheduled for Solidarity Day, June 19, 1968.

the other side there is another that says "God is Love" and one that reads: "Jesus Never Fails." In between there is a large black and white poster with the words "Black Is Beautiful" and "It's So Beautiful to Be Black."

Many of those who came to the church to sign up for the Poor People's Campaign are like Harry Smiley. He does not live in Marks. He comes from Lambert, Miss., a village less than seven miles away.

"I wasn't going until the other day," he explained in a manner that was almost too polite. "When these white people started beating people, I thought that something needs to be done about these things."

He was referring to an incident on Wednesday. In a fracas with the police, several students and a field staff organizer for the Southern Christian Leadership Conference were arrested and some teachers were reportedly beaten.

The Smiley youth said that he had quit school because his parents were no longer able to work and he had to help them. But the help that he could give was only meager.

"What we get for chopping cotton, you don't make nothing," he said. "People don't want to pay you over $2.50 a day. Sometimes you might make $3."

Recently he left the cotton fields for a job in a mill where, he said, he earned $1.25 an hour. "But that job didn't last long," he said. "I got laid off."

A week ago, he was called for his physical examination for the Army. "What am I going to do?" he said, repeating the question. "What can you do? If don't nothing happen, the Army or anything like that, I'm going to Washington."

The night before, many Negroes from Marks and the little towns around it had sat in the same church and listened late into the night as the Rev. Bernard Lee, a member of the Leadership Conference's executive staff, urged them to make the trip to Washington.

And before that they had listened to the Rev. James Bevel, one of the organization's chief community organizers.

"If President Johnson asks for your sons for two years," Mr. Bevel admonished the Negro parents, "you give them to him, and they die fighting in Vietnam."

Then, of the leadership conference, he said:

"We're in a terrible dilemma. We cannot come to your house and make your sons go with us. But when we ask for them you come telling us about some damn high school diploma and next year Johnson comes and gets your sons. We're going to develop a movement to save black people, and we're asking for your sons."

Mr. Bevel scoffed at the idea of remaining in school. "Graduate to what?" he fumed. "The West Side of Chicago, Harlem, East St. Louis, the unemployment lines of Memphis. What are they going to graduate? Is that what they're going to graduate to?"

Mrs. Sarah Ann Brown, a plump woman from Marks, said that she and her husband were taking four of their seven children with them.

"We've been going from the start," Mrs. Brown said. "We've been put off the plantation and discriminated against and everything and we're going to Washington."

A few minutes later Mrs. Brown began talking with the other women near the rear of Eudora Church, urging them to go on to Washington too.

"We want to go," one of the women said. "It's not that we don't want to go. But you know, some of us are afraid."

As reported in the previous article, the organizing effort was complicated by a series of confrontations that included the arrest of SCLC organizer and Mule Train Wagon Master Willie Bolden and the beating of several participants in a subsequent protest march. One of those beaten was Lydia McKinnon, then a schoolteacher in Marks. Ms. McKinnon, a native of Holly Springs, Mississippi, and a graduate of Jackson State University, had just begun her first teaching job, in Marks, that spring. Many students and teachers and a few town folk, including Ms. McKinnon, John and Laura Morris, and Johnny and Delores McGowen, demonstrated at the jail in protest of Bolden's arrest. When the sheriff and state troopers told them to leave, some of those involved sat down and refused to move.

When I spoke with her in February 1998, Ms. McKinnon, the only teacher assaulted during this protest, said:

I don't know what came over me. I don't think that I was courageous; it's just that for those few short moments, my life flashed before me. I had been in the segregated South all my life. White folks had the best of everything, and what we blacks were getting was worse than second best, and we were expected to do a good job with hardly anything. So, for that one crazy moment, I stood up for what I knew to be right, and with the butts of their guns and the heels of their boots, they knocked me unconscious for it. My parents asked me: "What got into you—don't you know you could have been killed?" Today, looking back on in it, I probably would not have done what I did; but as that young woman, I was just tired of the way we were being treated.

Lydia McKinnon was the first person I saw the first morning I woke up in Marks. It was only a couple of days since her beating, and I'll never forget how she looked. I had seen many people who'd been beaten in fights, and I'd been with and seen men beaten in civil rights demonstrations, but this was the first time I'd seen a woman who had been beaten, a fine young woman. Here we were, day one in Mississippi amidst my worst fears.

The Tuesday, May 7, 1968 edition of the *New York Times* reported the incident in an article titled "Negroes File Suit":

> Clarksdale, Miss., May 6—State and local law enforcement officials were accused in an attack on Negro demonstrators outside the Quitman County jail in nearby Marks last Wednesday.
>
> The suit entered in the United States District Court for the Northern District of Mississippi by lawyers for the NAACP Legal Defense and Educational Fund, Inc., seeks $550,000 damages for five teen-age girls, all Negroes.
>
> Named as defendants were Sheriff L. V. Harrison; L. C. Pride, a Negro serving as one of the three policemen in Marks; L. Y. Griffin, an officer of the Mississippi highway patrol; and two troopers identified only as "John Doe" and "Richard Doe."
>
> The plaintiffs were among some 300 young people who had marched to the jail to protest the arrest of Willie Bolden, an organizer of the Poor People's Campaign who had entered a Negro school in Marks to recruit for the march on Washington.

In general, members of both the executive branch and Congress viewed the Poor People's Campaign negatively and with suspicion—both politically and personally. Scattered acts of violence like the one just described added to the residual anxiety and fear from the series of riots in the wake of Dr. King's assassination. Indeed, it was common for those in power to urge both participants and observers to stay away, as was reported in the article, "Poor March Dangers Cited," by Robert S. Allen, in the Sunday, May 12 edition of the *Birmingham News*:

> Members of Congress are bluntly advising constituents to stay away from Washington during the impending "poor people's march."
>
> The legislators are warning of the possibility of a number of dangers—outbreaks of riots and violence, incendiary fires, which have continued to plague the capital since last month's costly disturbances following the slaying of Dr. Martin Luther King, and the spread of disease.

> The extraordinary development that members of Congress are telling their home folks not to come to Washington was vented by Sen. Karl Mundt, S.D., a ranking Republican on the powerful Appropriations and Foreign Relations Committee. He also disclosed that he is urging colleagues to do the same "because I fear we are headed for very serious trouble."
>
> "I have deemed it necessary, for the first time in my 30 years in Congress," Mundt said, "to tell the people of my state that if they have business in Washington, they should cancel it if possible. Also, if they must come, they should leave their wives and families at home, because until this so-called march is completed, visitors cannot feel safe in our capital city."
>
> President Johnson should make a personal appeal to the march leaders to drop their plans, Mundt declared, in the interest of both their professed cause and the security of the people in Washington. This view was echoed by Sen. Gordon Allott, R-Col., who contended the march will do more harm than good.
>
> "People have the right to petition," he said, "but they also have the right to do it in an orderly manner. When ten thousand, twenty thousand, thirty thousand or one hundred thousand people mass in one place to petition, it can hardly be called a petition. That is a demand. It is a demand that we bow our neck to the power represented by those people.
>
> "I do not propose to do that. For one thing, we must above all have law and order. The people who are coming here, no matter how well intentioned, are doing themselves a great disservice. I can listen to four or five people in my office, but I cannot listen to a crowd of ten or more thousand. And the same goes for other members of Congress."
>
> Sen. Strom Thurmond, R-S.C., cited testimony before the Senate Permanent Investigating Subcommittee that marchers will be armed.
>
> This admission came from Attorney General Ramsey Clark, who was questioned on the matter as follows: "Do you think that some of the people coming here will have guns?"
>
> Clark: "There will be people coming in with guns. There will be people already here who have guns. We have too many guns in this nation. That's one of the greatest difficulties. We urgently need to move effectively after them."

Although I don't believe there was a concerted effort to prevent the Poor People's Campaign from happening, it is clear that the climate reflected in this article encouraged local confrontations and a rash of acts of disruption and vandalism (some carefully orchestrated). The Mule Train was a target even before it got under way, as reported in the article, "30 Mules in March Back After Fleeing Through Cut Fence," in the Monday, May 13 edition of the *New York Times*:

> Marks, Miss., May 12 (UPI)—The leader of the mule train segment of the Poor People's March charged today that "a law enforcement officer" cut a corral fence shortly before dawn, allowing 30 mules to wander off.
>
> The mules were back by nightfall. Mule train participants found 28 of the animals, some of them as far as two miles away, and the other two wandered back for feed.
>
> "I was informed by a certain individual that he saw a law enforcement officer turn the mules out," said Willie Bolden, a staff worker for the Southern Christian Leadership Conference who is head of the mule train.
>
> He refused to identify the witness or the "law enforcement officer." When questioned, he said, "A law enforcement officer can be a county sheriff, a highway patrolman or even the FBI."
>
> Mr. Bolden also said that the mule train would leave Marks "at noon tomorrow." He said 16 wagons were ready to roll and all but five of the mules had been shod. Shoes will be put onto those five on the road, he said.
>
> The mule train has been beset by all kinds of trouble—lack of skilled blacksmiths and wagoneers, few tools, long distances to go for equipment, poor weather and mules stubbornly resisting the idea of shoes. Some mules had never been shod.

■ ■ ■

MARKS TO ATLANTA

After overcoming the difficulties of equipment and organization, the Mule Train set off from Marks on Monday, May 13, 1968, at 3:30 P.M.—about ten days later than initially scheduled. I had asked four young women, Shirley Brown, 15, Sadie Hill, 18, Denise Martin, 13, and Mary Will Tato, 21, to compile a roster of everyone who rode with us. The roster, though not exact, is quite accurate, at least for the stretch from Marks to Birmingham. It contains a range of information about each participant, including name, address, gender, age, emergency contact, and wagon in which traveling.[16]

For the first part of its journey about 115 people—roughly 100 poor people and 15 SCLC-provided staff—traveled with the Mule Train in its fifteen to twenty wagons. Thirty or more people assisted with driving the wagons, and another 15 or so served as volunteer staff. There were more than 40 women and almost 20 preteenagers. Ages ranged from 8 months to over 70 years, with more than half being between 17 and 30 years old. The participant roster kept changing as, all along the journey to Washington, new people would join and others would drop out.

Willie Bolden was the wagon master, whose basic responsibility was to see that the Mule Train successfully completed its journey, including overseeing the well-being of the people and animals involved. Daily feeding and sheltering of both were complicated and required a lot of advance arrangements. Special situations involving animals or equipment arose continuously leaving Mr. Bolden to scurry around making last minute adjustments.

Two cars and two trucks accompanied us. One truck carried hay and other feed for the mules and portable toilets; the second truck carried food for the participants, along with their suitcases and other personal belongings. The two cars had several functions: they were used for emergency transportation and communication, as well as for scouting the route for community support and receptivity. These vehicles would usually travel some miles down the road, await the Mule Train's arrival, and then move on.

Our route took us east across northern Mississippi and Alabama and then into Georgia. In the face of continuing delays and complications, it took more than a month to get from Marks to Atlanta, and as a result, the SCLC decided to load the entire Mule Train—people and equipment—onto a train from Atlanta to Alexandria, Virginia, just outside Washington, D.C. Upon arrival in Virginia, the equipment would be reassembled, and the Mule Train would cross the Potomac River for a dramatic Washington entrance.

The Mule Train's route and stops follow, and its route is shown on the map on the next page.

	May 13	Mule Train leaves Marks, MS, 3:30 P.M.
1st stop	May 14	8 miles west of Batesville, MS
2nd stop	May 15	Courtland, 5 miles south of Batesville, MS, on Highway 51
3rd stop	May 16	Grenada, MS—lost a horse and repaired wagons—4 days
4th stop	May 20	Duck Hill, MS
5th stop	May 21	Winona, MS
6th stop	May 22	Kilmichael, MS
7th stop	May 23	Eupora, MS—first encounter with legal trouble; stopped about a mile east of town by sheriff deputies
8th stop	May 24	Starkville, MS
9th stop	May 25	Columbus, MS
10th stop	May 26	Reform, AL—2 days
11th stop	May 28	Tuscaloosa, AL—2 days

---

[16] The appendix on pages 134 and 135 contains a complete roster of Mule Train participants.

MAP OF THE MULE TRAIN'S JOURNEY

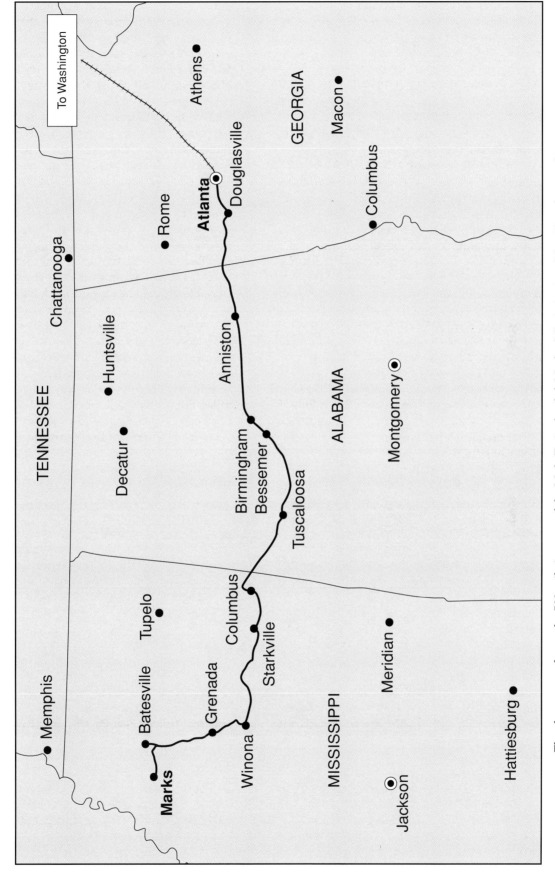

The above map shows the 500-mile journey of the Mule Train that left Marks, Mississippi on May 13 and arrived in Atlanta, Georgia, on June 15, 1968

12th stop	May 30	Cottondale, AL
13th stop	May 31	Bessemer, AL—loss of a wagon-1 day
14th stop	June 2	Birmingham, AL—3 days
15th stop	June 5	Anniston, AL—4 days
16th-	June 9-12	Records unclear as to exact
18th stops		locations and numbers of stops—most likely 2 to 3 over these 4 days
19th stop	June 13	Bremen, GA—stopped by state troopers and taken back to Douglasville
20th stop	June 14	Douglasville, GA—jailed in the National Guard Armory—1 day
21st stop	June 15	Atlanta, GA—rested; toured Atlanta and visited sites related to Dr. King; train arrangements for the evening of June 17—3 days
22nd stop	June 18	Alexandria, VA—boarded overnight train June 17 in Atlanta

All in all, the Mule Train traveled about five hundred miles in a month, averaging around twenty-five miles each of the days it was actually on the road and spending the remainder of the time at rest stops attending to enroute logistics.

The Mule Train was slowed down because the mules were unaccustomed to highways, paved roads and shoes, and the wagons were in frequent need of repair. Travel was not easy with the physical rigors of the journey and threats of confrontation with hostile whites and legal authorities. There were several incidents with a significant potential for violence, fortunately though, no major injuries or loss of life occurred. In one case, some of the wagons were shot at one night; in another, one of the scouting cars was stopped and its driver was threatened at knife point by a hostile group of whites. There were also legal delays, including arrests and near arrests. In Mississippi and Alabama, state troopers usually accompanied the Mule Train, which seemed to minimize local confrontations.

The daily task of feeding and sheltering the passengers and animals was complicated and required a lot of advance arrangements. Despite the planning by the wagon master and his staff, the preparation of its passengers, and the ongoing attention to logistics, the Mule Train faced adversity and challenge as it moved across the country. At the same time, it received support and encouragement all along the route. Not only did people—black and white, old and young—turn out to wish it well, but communities also organized to provide food and shelter for regular rest stops while individuals often ran out to press small contributions into our hands as we passed.

Each evening, when the Mule Train would stop for the day, activity would be in full swing. Food would be inventoried, distributed, and prepared; mules would be watered and fed; wagons and equipment

would be inspected and repaired; passengers would access their personal belongings; children would play; and staff would organize rallies, prayer meetings, and community support. All in all, there was an awesome amount of daily logistics to attend to as more than a hundred people traveled across the South.

The first articles appeared shortly after the Mule Train was under way. This article, "Mule Train on Way," is a UPI story from the Tuesday, May 14 edition of the *New York Times*:

> Marks, Miss., May 13 (UPI)—Fifteen mule-drawn wagons lurched off in a driving rain today as the mule train of the Poor People's March set off at last.
>
> About 80 persons huddled inside the canvas-covered wagons against the heavy downpour. The wagon caravan, delayed a week by various problems, stretched for 100 yards down Mississippi Highway 3. A highway patrol car with its blue light flashing led the way, and a massive traffic jam brought up the rear. The caravan is headed for Washington. It made 10 miles before stopping for the night.

The next article, "Hoof-Sore Already: Mule Train Limps Off, Bound for Alabama," by George Metz, is from the same day's *Birmingham News*:

> Batesville, Miss.,—An already hoof-sore Poor Peoples' mule train limped eastward today, finally on the way to Washington but its itinerary still uncertain.
>
> Willie Bolden, a Southern Christian Leadership Conference field worker and "wagon master" for the long-heralded mule train leg of the Washington Poor Peoples campaign, said late Monday the 15-wagon caravan was "headed for Alabama."
>
> "When we get there depends on how the mules and wagons hold up," he said.
>
> Several of the mules already were limping and the wagons appear rather rickety. The 29 mules and the 14 wagons were collected in Alabama around Huntsville. Two mules are pulling two wagons in tandem, with the extra mule hitched to the tailgate of one wagon.
>
> Bolden indicated the wagons may be dismantled when the march reaches Grenada, Miss., and the mules and wagons hauled by truck to Alabama, the next staging area for the Washington trek. A Highway Patrol official commanding some dozen patrolmen with the mule train said he had been told this was SCLCs tentative plan.
>
> Monday afternoon they were little more than

10 miles from where they pushed off, with Bolden in the true television wagon-train style shouting, "Move 'em out."

Three hours later the wagon train was barely out of sight of Marks with skittish young mules bucking, kicking at the traces and attempting to lunge off the highway at every field.

One team that bolted from the highway was grabbed by an elderly white man who was watching the procession pass. He and two Negro men, also elderly, quietly rearranged the team's harness, tightened the younger mule's traces, and the older Negro told the driver. "Let him feel it...he's gotta' know he's pulling something." One of the men called to the SCLC muleskinner, who was struggling with the reins, "Get a club and knock the hell out of him."

One minor incident marred the beginning of the march. The Highway Patrol arrested a march leader, Andrew W. Marrsett, charging him with obstructing a highway when he refused to move a car. An SCLC spokesman later stated Marrsett was angered when a patrolman called him "Boy." Bolden immediately retaliated by threatening to take the mule train to the jail and stay until Marrsett was released. "We're going to stay right here until we get him," Bolden threatened. However, Marrsett returned in company of two local Negro leaders before the wagons got rolling.

The wagon train rattled much of the way on the first leg of the journey through occasional rains, finally halting for the day at a Negro farm home.

The wagons were covered so it was difficult to count how many riders there were aboard them, but at one stop it appeared there were 65 or 70. After stopping for the day, most of the party went into Batesville and spent the night, though a few hardy souls spent the night with the wagons.

The following UPI article, "Georgia Yields on March Mule Train," from the Saturday, June 15 edition of the *Washington Post* relates to one of the last confrontations before reaching Atlanta:

Douglasville, Ga., June 14 (UPI)—Georgia state troopers halted the mule train segment of the Poor People's Campaign today and arrested 67 persons for trying to take wagons onto busy Interstate 20, but authorities later dropped the charges and opened the highway to the demonstrators.

Under the agreement worked out during a 90-minute meeting between Sheriff Caude Abercrombie and wagonmaster Willie Bolden the mule train will be allowed to travel along the emergency lane of Interstate 20 between the hours of 7 a.m. and 7 p.m. Saturday. Bolden told his 130 demonstrators to spend the night at the Zion Hill Baptist Church and be prepared to move out early Saturday.

"The charges have been dropped," Abercrombie announced as he emerged from the meeting.

GOVERNOR'S ORDERS

The troopers acting under orders from Gov. Lester Maddox, halted the mule train at an entrance ramp and arrested the 67 adults taking part in the demonstration.

[Thirty-two juveniles were quickly released but stayed with the adults, the Associated Press reported. The children included the 9-year-old son of Rev. Ralph David Abernathy, president of the Southern Christian Leadership Conference, and two sons of Hosea Williams, a top aide.]

Bolden said the mule train probably would reach Atlanta, 35 miles to the east, late Saturday. The wagons and the mules will be shipped to Washington later this weekend for a "grand entrance" into the capital.

Maddox said earlier that he ordered the action to "protect their own safety and welfare, as well as the safety of motorists" on Interstate 20, where the speed limit is 70 mph at some points. The demonstrators were charged with violating a law that prohibits use of non-motorized vehicles on the interstate highway.

OFFER REJECTED

Maddox offered to send flatbed trucks to pick up the mule train and transport it into Atlanta, or through the state. He also said he would be willing to provide an escort along any alternate route.

The mule train, which left Marks, Miss., in mid-May, spent last night at Douglasville and had hoped to reach Atlanta by tonight.

The arrests came as no surprise to Bolden, an official of the SCLC, which is sponsoring the Poor People's Campaign. He said authorities warned him last night not to try to use the interstate route.

He said since the mule train had used Interstate 55 in Mississippi and Interstate 20 in Alabama, he could see no justice in this decision and ordered the caravan to proceed along its chosen route.

When the 13-wagon train reached the ramp leading to I-20, it found scores of state and local police waiting. A State Highway Patrolman again told the demonstrators they could not proceed, and when the wagons defiantly moved out, authorities stepped in and made the arrests.

I remained with the Mule Train for about three weeks, from Marks until our arrival in Birmingham in early June. I then left to attend to family and personal matters and got back to Washington in time to greet the Mule Train upon its arrival in Virginia.

■ ■ ■

ATLANTA TO WASHINGTON

The Mule Train was far behind schedule when it reached Atlanta. In Washington, many of the key Poor People's Campaign events had already occurred and others were imminent, particularly Solidarity Day, June 19. Because the SCLC organizers were eager to have the Mule Train in Washington for what they saw as the culminating rally of the campaign, they decided to send it—participants, mules, wagons, and equipment—by train from Atlanta. On June 17, the participants boarded the train and traveled overnight, arriving in Alexandria the next morning. From there, Mule Train participants were dispersed for lodging throughout the area. Most of them stayed at a Methodist center outside the city, some joined family members or friends who were already at Resurrection City, and others stayed with local families. Based on location, they were bused daily to participate in the various Poor People's Campaign activities.

On June 19, the Mule Train people regathered, reassembled the wagons, and rehitched the mules; the caravan proceeded to the banks of the Potomac River, just across the river from Resurrection City and the Washington Monument.

The following articles address this final leg of the journey.[17] The first aritcle, "Poor to Follow Mule Train In Rail Car to Washington," by Walker Lundy, is from the Monday, June 17 edition of the *Atlanta Journal:*

> More than 100 participants in the mule train segment of the Poor People's Campaign will board the Southern Railway's crack passenger train, "The Southerner," Monday night for an all-night ride to a suburb outside Washington, D.C.
>
> Cost for 100-150 one-way coach tickets is between $2,000 and $3,000, which is being paid by the Southern Christian Leadership Conference.
>
> The poor people, who will be following by one day their mules and rickety wooden wagons, will join the bulk of the Poor People's Campaign in Resurrection City for "solidarity day" later this week.

---

[17] Though these first two articles indicate that the mules and wagons were shipped separately and by truck, I believe that they, as well as the passengers, were brought by train, as is stated in the subsequent articles.

The marchers were scheduled to visit the grave of Dr. Martin Luther King Jr. Monday afternoon and then go on a bus tour of Atlanta before leaving on the train at 7:10 p.m.

The decision to go by train apparently was made early Monday. SCLC officials were saying Sunday night that the group would travel to Washington by chartered bus.

The group, which includes about 30 children, had increased by a few dozen people early Monday with the arrival of a group from Huntsville, Ala., and the addition of some poor people from Atlanta.

SCLC officials told the Southern Railway that their civil rights organizations would purchase between 100 and 150 one-way coach fares sometime Monday afternoon, an official of the railroad said.

The railroad spokesman said it would require two or three extra cars on the train.

The SCLC already has shelled out $1,400 to send the mules and wagons ahead to the nation's capital.

The wagon train is supposed to reassemble in Alexandria, Va., just outside the nation's [capital] to prepare for the "solidarity day" march in Washington on Wednesday.

The mule train appeared to be suffering from financial problems Monday, but leaders denied that money was causing the disorganization.

"We're not at a point where we're hurting," said Bobby Nelson, one of the leaders of the group. "But I'm not saying we're a wealthy mule train either."

Travelers on the mule train, which clopped a weary 34-day path across the South, spent the weekend in Atlanta resting.

Marchers spent all day Friday in the National Guard Armory in Douglasville after being arrested in mass for trying to use Interstate Highway 20 to march into Atlanta.

Later after a compromise reached with the state patrol representing Gov. Lester Maddox, the wagon train left Douglasville at 3 a.m. Saturday and marched down the outside lane of the interstate into Atlanta. They arrived at 8:15 a.m. before traffic had become too heavy.

Douglasville is 30 miles west of Atlanta.

The next one, "Poor People's Mule Train Chugs Into Goal on Schedule," is from the Tuesday, June 18 edition of the *Atlanta Journal*:

> The Poor People Campaign's mule train— riding the last half of a 1,000-mile exodus out of Dixie aboard a railroad train—chugged into a

Virginia suburb of Washington Tuesday morning right on schedule.

Southern Railway reported 132 people detrained at Alexandria with 13 wagons and 34 mules sent on ahead Sunday.

The poor people were expected to spend Tuesday re-organizing and preparing for the expected mass march into the capital on "Solidarity Day" Wednesday.

Meanwhile, a group of more than 100 Atlantans were getting ready to leave here by chartered bus Tuesday night to join the Poor People's Campaign at Resurrection City and join in the march Wednesday.

A spokesman for the Metropolitan Atlanta Summit Leadership Congress, a conglomerate of Negro groups in Atlanta, said at least two bus loads of local poor people and students and at least two more bus loads of Atlantans paying their own way will depart here at 6 p.m. Tuesday for the all-night ride to Washington.

They are expected to return here Thursday morning.

Members of the mule train, the symbolic part of the campaign conceived by Dr. Martin Luther King Jr. before his death, left here Monday night 30 minutes late on "The Southerner," Southern Railway's New Orleans-to-New York passenger train. They arrived about 7:35 a.m. Tuesday, the railroad reported.

They spent the weekend in Atlanta resting. Monday, they visited the grave of Dr. King where they held a short memorial service and then toured the city by chartered bus. The mules and wagons left by train Sunday for Alexandria.

The Mule Train began 38 days ago in Marks, Miss., and clopped its way through the heart of the Southland, picking up poor people as it went. It marched through Mississippi, Alabama and into Georgia.

By the time they arrived in Atlanta early Saturday morning, the train members had covered more than 500 miles—about half the distance to Washington.

The Southern Christian Leadership Conference, the Atlanta-based civil rights organization sponsoring the Poor People's Campaign, said the mule train lived off donations along the way.

The final article on the last leg of the journey, "Rickety Mule Train Plods in to Wait for March," by Paul W. Valentine, is from the Wednesday, June 19 edition of the *Washington Post*:

The Poor People's mule train rumbled to the banks of the Potomac yesterday on the last leg of its trek from Mississippi and prepared to join the "Solidarity Day" march in Washington today.

The 13 wagons, some of them canting perilously on rickety frames, traveled north from Alexandria on the George Washington Memorial Parkway to a National Park Service maintenance area near the west end of the Memorial Bridge in Virginia, where the mules were bedded down for the night. The six-mile trip took three hours.

Traffic was tied up behind the mule train as Alexandria, Arlington County and Park Police shepherded the group along in the curb lane on the northbound side of the Parkway.

The train moved at a steady gait except at two points—once when a wheel rim broke off a wagon and had to be fixed and later when an auto driver behind the last wagon began shouting angrily and found himself surrounded by about 35 youths from the train.

The youths dared him to get out of his car. A Park Police sergeant moved in, dispersed the youths and directed the driver into the open lane around the mule train.

The wagons and mules, which along with about 80 persons made the 600-mile trek from Marks, Miss., to Atlanta Ga., were shipped by train to Alexandria Monday.

The mules were held in an improvised corral at the Southern Railway freight depot near Duke and South Henry Streets in Alexandria Monday night.

Veterinarians examined the animals—28 mules and four horses—and found five so lame or harness-burned that Humane Society officials arranged to have them shipped by trailer to a 144-acre Society farm in Waterford, Va., 35 miles away.

Veterinarian D. W. Francis of Arlington said that despite the lameness and burns, "they seem to be in good shape." He said he gave penicillin shots to four animals.

Mule skinners reassembled the 13 wagons at the depot, hitched the animals, and moved out at 2:50 p.m.

A Southern Railway spokesman said the cost of shipping the wagons and mules from Atlanta was $1500. "We had a hard time finding stock cars for the mules," he said. "We haven't shipped livestock in years."

Early yesterday, 127 persons accompanying the mule train arrived in Alexandria by train from Atlanta. More than 40 of them had joined the train there. The women and children went to the Northern Virginia Baptist Center in Gainesville,

Va., 28 miles away, for food and lodging, while the men remained to help with the mule train.

In some ways the Mule Train never escaped its logistical complications, and the mules and wagons did not cross the river for the Solidarity Day rally but arrived later as reported in this UPI article, "After an 1,100-Mile Trip, Mule Train Misses Rally," appearing in the Thursday, June 20 edition of the *New York Times*:

> Washington, June 19 (UPI)—The mule train that became a symbol of the Poor People's Campaign during an 1,100-mile, five-week journey missed taking part in the rally today.
>
> The Rev. Andrew Young, first vice president of the Southern Christian Leadership Conference, said the last leg of the mule train—from Arlington National Cemetery to the Lincoln Memorial—was postponed because it would have caused too much "confusion" in the march.
>
> The mule train left Marks, Miss., on May 13 and arrived in Atlanta last Saturday. The wagons and mules and the people bringing them traveled from Atlanta to the Washington area by train.

The complications of caring for the mules also continued into Washington as reported in Carol Honsa's article, "Park Police Caring for March Mules," in the Sunday, June 23 edition of the *Washington Post*:

> U.S. Park Police are feeding and watering the mules which hauled the Poor People's Campaign mule train into Washington. Campaign officials apparently made no arrangements for feeding the animals.
>
> Campaign mule drivers have been looking in on them but have brought them no food, according to a team of Park Police tending to the 24 mules and three horses in a Park Service enclosure near Arlington Cemetery.
>
> The Arlington Animal Welfare League is supplying food for the animals and the Arlington County Fire Department is providing water.
>
> Police said at least two officers from the mounted patrol are stationed around the clock to tend the teams.
>
> "We're not supposed to be feeding them, but we're doing it as a courtesy to the mules," said Pvt. Edward B. Cutshaw, who was busy distributing hay to the animals.
>
> "They left them here and we had to take over," said Pvt. George C. DuLaney.
>
> Arthur Hale, Animal Welfare League humane agent, said the League is now supplying 300 pounds of grain and 12 bales of hay daily to feed the "guests."

> Hale said he had also been bringing salves and medicine for animals suffering the effects of their long trip. Several mules were seen with raw wounds on their necks and legs where they had been cut by collars and wagon traces.
>
> Pvt. James E. Thomas pointed out a pony suffering an infection between the shoulder blades where a saddle had rubbed.
>
> Some of the mules are 20 to 30 years old, he said.
>
> Hosea Williams, a Campaign leader, disputed the police version. He said he gave the mule skinners $147 for feed for the animals for Wednesday, Thursday and Friday and an additional $60 yesterday.

I was curious about what eventually happened to the mules, so in early March 1998, with help from the National Park Service, I contacted each of the three mounted police identified in the story who had been assigned to watch over the mules in Washington: Officers Edward B. Cutshaw, George C. DuLaney, and James E. Thomas. All are now retired—Cutshaw lives in Texas, and DuLaney and Thomas in suburban Maryland, just outside Washington. Each recounted fond memories of the mules and remembered them as being in reasonably good shape given the length and rigors of the journey just completed. One said:

> Our job was to look after the mules, and we found ourselves bonding with them. We cared for all of them—some had sores inflicted by the strains of their harnesses. After a few days of this care—feeding, watering, and grooming the mules—the bond grew stronger, and we found ourselves doing far more than our jobs required.

According to the officers, when the summer of protest had ended, some of the mules were taken to a farm in Columbia, Maryland, owned by the Revere family; others were taken to central Virginia and put out to pasture. I have been unable to learn what happened to the wagons.

■ ■ ■

RESURRECTION CITY

As indicated earlier, the SCLC anticipated that the Poor People's Campaign would continue for an extended time period—until the federal government demonstrated through resources and leadership that it had understood and was willing to take action to come to grips with the problem of poverty in America. A key strategic element was to have poor people from around the country come to Washington, D.C., and remain there for the duration of the campaign. They would establish a temporary residential community in the capital and would spearhead the petitioning. They would all be trained in nonviolence and would organize the much larger numbers of people who would come together for selected demonstrations. The SCLC was seeking a location that would basically demand that these people would be encountered by congresspeople daily, so that the legislators would be unable to escape the real faces of poverty.

The National Park Service issued the SCLC permits to establish this settlement in West Potomac Park, on the National Mall, along the Reflecting Pool between the Lincoln and Washington Monuments. Based on planning and building advice from four architects, James Goodell, Ken Jadin, Tunney Lee, and John Wiebenson, volunteers prefabricated plywood residences with canvas sides at a church center in suburban Maryland. There were at least two designs, one for families and one for unrelated individuals.[18]

Once the materials were transported to the Mall, campaign participants, usually from the same geographical area and working as a unit, raised their own residential sections along the several streets that had been laid out. Several communal facilities— toilets, a shower hall, a clinic, a day care area, a dining hall, an office for city administration—were also put up, and ditches were dug for water and plumbing lines.[19]

The site was named Resurrection City as a symbol of rebirth from the depths of oppression and hopelessness; its first residents arrived on May 12. It was dedicated the next day—the same day the Mule Train left Marks, Monday, May 13, 1968. Though many of the Poor People's Campaign participants were housed in other group and family settings throughout the metropolitan area, more and more people took up residence in Resurrection City. At its peak in June, there were more than seven thousand people in facilities initially anticipated for fifteen hundred to three thousand. In addition, May and June rainfalls were far heavier than average, and for much of the time, Resurrection City was a veritable quagmire, dirty and slippery, with mud holes one could fall into. With its minimal living conditions, the weather, overcrowding, undercover agents, troublemakers, and conflicts among political and social constituencies, Resurrection City soon became virtually a metaphor for the very conditions being protested by the campaign.

[18] I am indebted to John Wiebenson for the information about designing and building Resurrection City.
[19] Unfortunately, the contractor, fearing liability for any inadvertent damage from tapping into underground water lines, neither connected the water nor refilled the ditches, and when the rains came, these ditches proved a major hazard for the temporary city's residents.

While rallies, demonstrations, and lobbying took place through May and June, the situation in Resurrection City continued to deteriorate. Meeting after Robert Kennedy's assassination on June 5, its leaders decided to bring this part of the Poor People's Campaign to a close, emphasizing the gains made. The Solidarity Day Rally for Jobs, Peace, and Freedom was scheduled for "Juneteenth," June 19, an important date for African-Americans that represents the day by which word of Lincoln's Emancipation Proclamation reached slaves in the Deep South. Solidarity Day would be the summer's final major event, after which the SCLC would begin to bus home the remaining participants.

Solidarity Day was a success with more than fifty thousand people participating in the rally in front of the Lincoln Memorial. Many people left for home immediately afterward, yet many stayed on despite the conditions in Resurrection City. There were occasional confrontations with the Washington police, and one night, in retaliation for an incident involving motorists near the Mall, police began to teargas the entire community causing a situation that only narrowly missed exploding into major violence.

Even though the campaign's leaders had decided to close down Resurrection City and had arranged with the Department of the Interior to provide a few additional days for an orderly exit, on June 25, with several dozen people still remaining on site, the National Guard, along with local law enforcement units, closed Resurrection City. They surrounded and removed with force the remaining people and subsequently leveled the ground.

The first of the following articles, "'City' of Poor Begun in Capital: Abernathy Vows to 'Plague Pharaohs of Nation' for Help Against Poverty," by Ben A. Franklin, from the Tuesday, May 14 edition of the *New York Times*, takes us back to Resurrection City's dedication:

> Washington, May 13—The Rev. Ralph David Abernathy today dedicated "Resurrection City, U.S.A.," with a vow "to plague the Pharaohs of this nation with plague after plague until they agree to give us meaningful jobs and a guaranteed annual income."
>
> Construction of the "city" of plywood shelters near the Lincoln Memorial began at once. They will house 3,000 participants in the Poor People's Campaign who are coming here from various parts of the nation.
>
> Mr. Abernathy pledged again to conduct a nonviolent protest "to arouse the conscience of the nation." But he said that "we cannot give you any other further guarantee" that the city will not be disrupted by massive acts of civil disobedience.

"Unlike the previous marches which have been held in Washington," he said, "this march will not last a day, or two days, or even a week. We will be here until the Congress of the United States decide that they are going to do something about the plight of the poor people by doing away with poverty, unemployment and underemployment in this country."

If necessary, Mr. Abernathy told a jammed outdoor news conference, "we will stay until Congress adjourns.

"And then we're going to go where Congress goes, because we have decided that there will be no new business until we first take care of old business," he said.

This was an apparent allusion to the plans of the Southern Christian Leadership Conference to "plague" the Republican and Democratic National Conventions, to which many members of Congress will go in August. The Southern Christian Leadership Conference, headed by the Rev. Dr. Martin Luther King Jr. before his murder on April 4 and by Mr. Abernathy now, is sponsoring the Poor People's Campaign.

Mr. Abernathy, wearing blue denim workman's clothes, which are the uniform of the Southern civil rights movement, drove a ceremonial nail and pounded ineffectually at a 2-by-4 stake with a light carpenter's hammer to begin the erection of about 600 dwellings for the poor in the glade near the Lincoln Memorial.

The plywood "city" in West Potomac Park, one of the most beautiful spots in the formal Federal area of the city—and one of the noisiest because of the jet aircraft leaving Washington National Airport—will receive this week 3,000 temporary residents, the population allowed under an Interior Department permit.

Demonstrations are to begin next week. They are to reach a climax with a "massive invasion of hundreds of thousands" of one-day demonstrators and sympathizers on Memorial Day, Thursday, May 30.[20]

The civil disobedience, if it comes, will presumably begin in June. The campsite permit, which is renewable if the Government chooses to extend it, expires on Sunday, June 16.

Mr. Abernathy hinted today that before then he would seek an appointment with President Johnson.

"I don't want to give all our strategy," he said, "but let me say this—we are going to leave no stone unturned. We will make no deal, however. Whatever we do, it's going to be through nonviolent demonstrations."

[20] This demonstration was rescheduled for June 19, as the Solidarity Day Rally for Jobs, Peace, and Freedom.

Mr. Abernathy is scheduled to confer informally on legislative goals Wednesday with a number of Congressmen. The conveners of the meeting are a bipartisan group of sympathetic Senators and Representatives.

As each stroke of Mr. Abernathy's hammer fell on the symbolic stake, driven in advance into the turf of a 16-acre clearing, 500 Negroes cried "Freedom." They were members of a "construction battalion," the vanguard of the poor that arrived here yesterday from Mississippi by bus.

Then the workers began assembling the prefabricated sections of the A-frame shelters. By nightfall about 100 had been completed. The work continued under floodlights.

Contractors began installing electrical, sewer and water lines.

Mr. Abernathy began the ceremony in the West Potomac Park by leading the singing of "We Shall Overcome." He led a separate chorus of "white and black together," "red and black together" or "brown and black together" for each of the groups to be represented in the campaign—poor whites, American Indians, Puerto Ricans, and Mexican-Americans, as well as Negroes.

In a symbolic rejection of the Government authority through which they obtained their campsite permit, leaders of the Southern Christian Leadership Conference have several times in recent days brought Indians to public events to ask them, as "the people who were here first," for permission to use Federal land. Today was no exception.

Mr. Abernathy summoned Linda Aranayko, a pretty, 20-year-old member of the Creek tribe from Oklahoma, to his side and asked her, "Is it all right if we use this land?" When she replied, "Yes," he said, "I declare this to be the site of our new city of hope, Resurrection City, U.S.A."

The first 8-by-20-foot plywood dwelling to go up is to be occupied by Mrs. Minnie Lee Hill, 40 years old, of Marks, Miss., who came here with eight of her 12 living children. She has had 17 children, she said. Five of them died in infancy.

The following opinion piece, from Drew Pearson and Jack Anderson's *Washington Merry-Go-Round* in the June 15 edition of the Washington Post, "It's Time for the Poor to Go Home," is representative of the increasingly negative media stance as the Poor People's Campaign continued:

For their own good and the good of the country, the Poor People's March should now fold up Resurrection City and go home.

In the first place, they have achieved some of their goals. A $5 billion housing bill has been passed; more than $200 million in surplus food has been earmarked.

In the second place, the Poor People have reached the point of diminishing returns. If they stay longer, they may hurt what they have accomplished.

No group in years have been treated so generously by the Federal Government, which allowed them to camp on a public park, and by the churches of the city and by most of the residents in Washington. The churches opened up their doors, women made thousands of sandwiches, people contributed blankets, the Hechinger hardware stores contributed lumber at cost, many grocery store chains contributed food.

The public park adjacent to the Lincoln Memorial has been churned up by bulldozers and the daily wear of several thousand feet to a point where it will take at least a year to restore the grass. Poor People's marshals, acting with the officiousness which they objected to on the part of Birmingham police, have even barred picture taking, saying, "These are private homes," though of course they are located on land belonging to all the taxpayers.

Negro newsmen have been beaten and pushed around. The Supreme Court, which has done more for racial equality than any institution in history, had its windows broken. The Negro population of Washington has suffered economically because summer business is down, tourism is off. Greyhound Bus alone cancelled $200,000 worth of bus trips to Washington. This hurt the Negro population of Washington first.

All this has been taken with considerable forbearance by the citizens of Washington.

Negro newsmen have been the most critical. "The Washington press," wrote William Raspberry, widely read Negro columnist of the *Washington Post*, "has, if anything, been too kind. If more of the internal strife, lack of control and poor discipline had been reported, there might have been more pressure to set things right."

Louis Lomax, national Negro columnist, has reported on "absentee leadership" of "a city of chaos" and told of a "night of violence, disruption and non-leadership that easily could have spilled over into Washington itself."

He reported how "several carloads of middle-class women, Negro and white, who arrived with food and clothing were brusquely turned away by marshals whose lack of knowledge manifested itself in surliness and incredible rudeness."

Lomax described Resurrection City as "completely unsafe, a jungle at night." And as early as May 25 he called it a "city falling apart, dangerously so."

It is now June 15 and Resurrection City, abandoned by a majority of the Poor People, should fold up and go home.

SECTION 2
VOICES FROM THE MULE TRAIN: PERSPECTIVES FROM PARTICIPANTS

INTRODUCTION

The next section gives voice to some of the individuals who were directly involved in the Mule Train—participants, organizers, and observers. Two of these conversations occurred in 1968, almost thirty years ago and the rest, more recently, while preparing this book. This provided me an opportunity to get back in touch with people and reflect on our shared experiences three decades later.

This section contains transcripts of the following.[22]

There are two interviews with Bertha Johnson Luster. The first was conducted in May 1968 and the second in October 1997. Mrs. Luster was a Mule Train participant from Marks who is now a member of the 30th Anniversary Celebration Committee.

An interview with Lee Dora Collins was conducted in October 1997 and provides a retrospective look through the eyes of a Mule Train participant whose life typifies to me many from the Delta.

An interview with Joan Cashin and Myrna Copeland was conducted in May 1968. They were participants from Alabama, one black and one white, who helped in the Mule Train preparations.

There are written comments by John Cashin. Dr. Cashin, who helped the SCLC organize the Mule Train, provided these comments in February 1998 after talking with me and reviewing the 1968 interview with his wife and Mrs. Copeland.

Following several brief contacts, I interviewed Willie Bolden, the former SCLC organizer and Mule Train wagon master, by telephone on February 28, 1998.

Finally there are written comments by Jean Smith Freas. Mrs. Freas, then a journalist covering the Mule Train for television, provided these comments in January 1998 following an earlier conversation between us.

---

[22] In 1968, I had interview transcripts prepared from cassette field recordings. Because they were unedited and I've been unable to locate the original tapes, I've modified the comments minimally for clarity and continuity. All interviewees, except Mrs. Joan Cashin who has passed, have had the opportunity to review what is here.

■ ■ ■

INTERVIEWS WITH BERTHA JOHNSON LUSTER

I first interviewed Bertha Johnson (now Luster) on May 14, 1968, while we were riding a Mule Train wagon, on our second day out, enroute from Marks to Batesville, Mississippi. Mrs. Luster still lives in Marks and is a member of the 30th Anniversary Mule Train Celebration Committee. It was she who contacted me in September 1997 to discuss the event and ultimately invited me to participate by curating the exhibit on which this book is based.

At the time of the Poor People's Campaign, Bertha Johnson was working for the SCLC office in Marks. She assisted by maintaining rosters of who participated, who traveled on the Mule Train, who traveled by bus, when people came and went, and where they stayed in Washington. She was also responsible for getting bus tickets for people to return home, and as such was among the last people to leave Washington when the campaign closed down.

I'm indebted to Mrs. Luster for her generosity in sharing with me her Mule Train records and memorabilia. Her cooperation has been invaluable in developing both the exhibit and the book.

* * *

Mrs. Johnson, what is your maiden name
My maiden name is Burres.

How old are you, where were you born, and who were your parents?
I am twenty-eight years old and was born in Quitman County (MS) on the Graver's Plantation. My daddy's name is Nelson Burres. He was born on the McDowell Plantation in Batesville (MS) in Panola County. He will be fifty this December. When he was twenty-two, he married my momma, Parlee Hicks Burres. She was seventeen and was born near Yazoo City (MS) on the Blackton Plantation. She has eight children—one she had before she met my father.

How old were you when you got married, who was he, and where was he from?
I got married in 1956—I was sixteen and my husband was seventeen. His name is Charles Johnson. He came to Marks with his father who was an evangelist preacher. I liked him right off and things just sort of happened. I dropped out of high school and Charles went into the air force.

Did you travel with him?
I sure did. It was my opportunity to get out of Marks. We went to France then came back to Travis Air Force Base in California. We stayed there for about five years, and by then we had four children. In 1963 we

Terence Johnson and his mother, Bertha Johnson Luster, standing in front of their home
MARKS, MISSISSIPPI, JANUARY 1998

went to England and were stationed on Weathersfield Air Force Base. My son Terrence was born there.

When you left England, where did you go?
I came back to my husband's home in Memphis (TN). That's where my husband got in trouble and split for Chicago. He wasn't sending any money back so the kids and I went to Chicago to live with my sister. I got a job working in a company that made men's belts. I stayed in Chicago for about a year. Lots of Mississippi folks were in Chicago, but most of them were just as poor as me. Things got pretty rough up there with hardly any help from my husband, and I had trouble making ends meet. I decided to come back home to Marks—it was even worse back there, but at least I was around family.

What did you do once you got back to Marks?
I first tried to get on public assistance, but they told me to go back to Chicago. Then Reverend Ingram asked me to do some secretarial work for the NAACP and the Voter's League. Then some people hooked me up with SCLC folks like Roosevelt Archie, R. B. Cottonreader, Bobby Nelson, and Eugene Marrisette.

How did you first hear about the Mule Train?
Through the SCLC field-workers. They were in here organizing for the Poor People's Campaign. Lots of folks were signing up to ride the buses to Washington. Willie Bolden was one of those people who went to the schools to talk to the teachers and the children and tell them about their rights. The sheriff found out about it and warned him to stop. When he wouldn't, they locked him up. Old Sheriff L. V. Harrison, that was his name. He didn't have enough deputies, so he called in the state troopers.

Explain to me what happened.
We had decided to go up to the jail to protest them locking up Willie Bolden. But Willie got word to me not to be part of the protest because it was more important for me to run the SCLC office than to be in jail. My job was to call Atlanta (GA, SCLC headquarters) and let them know about the trouble that was going on. He had given me telephone numbers for Hosea Williams, Andrew Young, and Walter Fauntroy who was in Washington, D.C.

While you were doing all of this, what were the protesters doing?
Some were running, and others, who didn't run, were getting their butts beaten.

Do you remember anyone in particular?

There were all of these students and some teachers. The teachers were up front, and the sheriff told them and the children to go back to school. He said that they shouldn't be concerned about Willie Bolden. He told them that they shouldn't get mixed up with outside troublemakers.

What happened?
Well you see, I wasn't right there when all of this happened, but from what they tell me, it went something like this. There was the sheriff and the state troopers all lined up, and when they told everyone to move, most did, but a few just sat down. That kind of made them real mad for black people to disobey a white man. One of those who sat down was Lydia McKinnon.[22] She got beat up pretty bad. Some say that she was kicked in the face and hit with rifle butts, but she refused to move.

Was this the first time that the people here in Marks protested?
Well, I couldn't say that it was the first time, but I do know that after the sheriff and state troopers beat those folks up, a lot of newspeople came in here. It wasn't long after that that all you people started coming in here getting ready for this southern caravan. They put these big tents over there on the other side of the railroad track. People started coming from everywhere to go on the bus or the Mule Train. You see, after they killed Dr. King, many of these folks found some courage they didn't know they had before. They just decided that they wanted their freedom and they wanted it now.

When people say that, what do you think that they mean?
They are tired of being on these plantations—being poor and not being given their equal rights. So we're going to Washington to let them folks up there know that it is time they treated us right and we ain't gonna take it no more.

I didn't interview Mrs. Johnson again during the Mule Train or while she was in Washington. We spoke again when I went to Marks in October 1997.

Mrs. Luster, did going to Washington on the Mule Train meet your expectations, and has it made a difference in your life?
I gained the courage to speak up for myself. I got married young, you see, and the first time I spoke up to my husband I almost had a nervous breakdown. He was not very secure and had trouble coping with life, so he sort of dominated me—you understand what I mean? SCLC taught me that there is no harm

in speaking up. That's the only way you can let people know what you think and feel. Now there's another side to this speaking-up business. I also discovered that sometimes when you speak up for others they might leave you hanging out there by yourself. For me, the big lesson from the Mule Train was not what we got in Washington, but what we learned and gained by sticking together to get to Washington. In Washington things fell apart. There were rumors that some of the SCLC staff had sold us out before our demands were met. Just before they tore down Resurrection City (about June 25), many of the people from Mississippi had already started to go back. It was my job to help them get bus tickets. My children and me were among the last ones to leave, finally doing so on July 20, 1968.

What happened when the people who had been on the Mule Train came back to Mississippi?
Well, all the Mule Train people weren't from Mississippi. We picked up folks along the way in Alabama and Georgia. Some people didn't come back home: a few stayed in Washington, some came back to Atlanta, but mostly all of the people from Marks came back. 'Til this day a lot of folk won't talk about the Mule Train.

What do you think is the reason for this?
Well, looking back on it now, I can understand how we were expecting too much. Some of the people who stopped in Resurrection City didn't like the fact that some of SCLCs staff were staying in fancy air conditioned hotels. You got to remember we were kind of naive. The SCLC leaders told us we were going to Washington to demand that our government give us forty acres and a mule. Now we weren't stupid. We knew that we weren't going to get forty acres and a mule, but we did believe the part about being able to get better jobs and a better education for our children. This would allow us to have a better lifestyle. But most of us came back here to the same old same old. Over the years change has come, but it has been very slow. You see, you'd be hard-pressed today to find people who were on the Mule Train. They all had to leave here to find work; there wasn't anything here.

What did you do when you got back to Marks?
Well, I first got a job working on a compress in a cotton gin. It wasn't much, but that's all that was available. I had my children to raise and got no help from their father. Then for a few years, I taught reading and writing in a literacy program. After that, I worked for a while in a girdle factory in Batesville.

Did you ever see your husband, Charles Johnson, again?
I heard about him, but he kept moving around so that the courts could not catch up to him for child

---

22 See pp. 30 and 100 for Ms. McKinnon's picture and reflections on this incident.

support. When I was thirty-one, I married my second husband. He was eight years younger than I was. It turns out he wasn't any good either. He started spending more time with my seventeen-year-old cousin, Betty, with whom he ended up having two children. After the children were born, he let her go. In 1991, I turned fifty and I married David Luster. We are now separated. He turned out to be unfaithful too. After this mess, I decided that I am just finished with men. You see I've been unlucky in love, I've worked for a telephone company, and I've worked as a bus driver for Head Start. Now, I just live with my youngest son in my daddy's old shotgun house. It's not easy, but we're getting by—we got each other.

What do you think about the 30th Anniversary Mule Train Celebration planned for May 1998?
Well, just working on the planning of it has made me feel young again. They were really some exciting times when the Mule Train went to Washington. Most young people around here today don't think that something like the Mule Train leaving here really happened. But I am really excited about folks knowing our history and that we did something that a lot of people thought couldn't be done. We made it to Washington.

■ ■ ■

INTERVIEW WITH LEE DORA COLLINS

I interviewed Lee Dora Collins, a Mule Train participant from Marks, on October 24, 1997, at her home. Mrs. Collins, now retired, still lives in Marks, where she is raising her grandson. In many ways, her life seems to me representative of poor Delta women of her generation, and this interview sheds additional light on the conditions in the South at the time of the Mule Train. Mrs. Collins was looking forward to celebrating the 30th Anniversary and enthusiastic in her encouragement of both the exhibit and the book.

* * *

Mrs. Collins, how old are you, and where were you born?
I was born in 1926 on the Bruce Jones Plantation near Belzoni in Humphrey County (MS).

Who were your parents?
My mother's name was Lula Hart (1907–82). She was born on a plantation near Inverness in Sunflower County (MS). My father's name was John Miller (1882–1971). He was born on a plantation in the hill country around Utica, in Hinds County (MS).

Where were you raised?
Well, as I recollect, we moved about quite a bit. It just depended on how we were treated. If we were treated good we'd stay longer, but we were always looking

for a better way to make it. So we lived on the Bruce Jones Plantation until I was four or five years old. Then we moved to a plantation near Swiftown in Leflore County (MS). I think the plantation had the same name as the town.

Where did you go to school?
Well first thing you have to understand, we only went to school when we weren't needed in the field, and then we had to walk five or six miles to the Rolling Wall School which was in a church on the Charlie Nickel Plantation.

Did you stay on this plantation?
No. A few years later Daddy moved us to the Allen Cobes Plantation in Itta Bena (MS). We stayed there for two years. Things really didn't work out too well for us there, so Daddy moved us again. This time we went to Miss Moorhead's plantation three miles below Greenwood in Leflore County. Along about then, I can remember things really well. We had left one bad situation and then moved to another one that wasn't much better.

What do you mean?
Well this is the way it was. We worked all year long and could barely break even. We knew well how things worked. We always had a cow to get milk and butter, and it was always one of us children's jobs to stake the cow in the ditches along the highway for grazing. We always raised a big garden to can food to

Lee Dora Collins in her front yard
MARKS, MISSISSIPPI, JANUARY 1998

last us through the winter. We raised our own hogs and chickens. We seldom got much on the books. Generally the plantation owner provided necessities from the commissary store such as syrup, sugar, flour, and sometimes a side of pork or a bag of beans or cloth for clothing. Arrangements were also made if items were needed from the general store. Tenants seldom received cash, and any items that were put on the books were deducted after tenants had gotten their cotton crop in. Now here we all were on Miss Moorhead's plantation. She gave each family three hundred dollars, and you see, it just wasn't fair. We hadn't borrowed nowhere near what everybody else had but she still only gave us three hundred dollars for the year. Told us that the price of cotton was really low that year and that's all we were going to get. Some years they would tell us that we didn't break even and didn't give us nothing. There was nothing you could do about it.

When did you get married?
He was twenty-nine years old and lived on the same plantation. I was fifteen, and we got married when I was sixteen. Together we had fifteen children and raised sixteen in total. We lived on Miss Moorhead's plantation for six or seven years. A friend of ours was doing pretty good on a plantation in Missouri, and when he came home for a visit he made it sound so good that we moved up there. My daughter Clara was born there. We stayed a little better than a year, but it wasn't really any better than it was in Mississippi, so we came back to Miss Moorhead's plantation for about another three years. Then we moved to Louis Fancher's plantation in Leflore County. Mr. Fancher was one of the best people that we sharecropped for. Some years we cleared fifteen hundred to two thousand dollars. He treated us real nice and encouraged us to buy our own property. We started paying down on the plot here in Marks where I live now. When we first moved to Marks, we sharecropped for two years for Mr. Holliway Hinscliffer. His plantation is right here in Quitman County. It was during this time that we first got involved in civil rights activities with the NAACP. In those days you had to sneak around and have your meetings in secret.

Why was that?
They would lock you up, beat you, or even something worse. It was really dangerous being involved in the civil rights business, but we did it anyway. I wanted to see things change for my children. We all worked hard all the time. During one cotton-picking season on our next plantation in Penola County (MS) on the Bruce Allen Plantation, my husband and I had ten of our sixteen children in the field. When the weevils didn't get the cotton and we had a good crop, we could average between eight and eleven bales a year. But even with ten children helping us, we still weren't clearing three thousand dollars a year. This was one of the reasons we knew civil rights was so important. It was the only hope we had.

In the early 1960s we stopped sharecropping. My husband was a pretty good mechanic so he fixed cars, lawnmowers, and the like around the house. He also cut some pulpwood and worked at the sawmill. Me and the children would do day work chopping and picking cotton and pulling corn. We worked ten to twelve hours a day for three dollars. Things were hard, but with the Lord's good blessings, we made it through and I'm proud to say that we were never on welfare. But we were still tired of being poor no matter how hard we worked. We just weren't getting our just do. I had been hearing about marches for a long time. In the early 1960s Reverend Allen of New Dora Church and Preacher Malone of Unity Baptist Church took six of my children to a march over there in Alabama. My third child, Clara, was a secretary for the SCLC, and they trained on how to register people to vote. You see they used to make it real hard for us to register. Some time in late 1967 or early 1968—I don't remember exactly—Dr. Martin Luther King and his people came right here to Marks. First he came to my church, the Silent Grove Baptist Church. When he walked down the aisle, something came over me. You see, a Christian can feel a Christian, and this day, his presence touched my spirit like he was God-sent. I just knew our time had come. We were bound for freedom. He was talking about this Poor People's Campaign business. Then he went to New Dora Methodist Church. That's where the children were and he wept. The SCLC began to organize in this whole area for people to go to Washington. Some was gonna go on the bus caravan and the rest on the Mule Train.

That April, Dr. King was murdered right there in Memphis. Before they killed him, it was hard to get people to go to Washington, but afterwards folk came from everywhere. SCLC workers Rev. Willie Bolden and R. B. Cottonreader were around here organizing. Willie Bolden turned the schools out and the kids marched to the courthouse. One of the teachers, Ms. Lydia McKinnon, was beat pretty bad. Folks started running everywhere and an ambulance came. Some went to the hospital and others were taken to jail; then everybody showed up. Never saw so many newspeople in all my life. They were everywhere. SCLC put up some big tents and started putting together the wagons and the mules. My thirteen-year-old son, O. C., was one of the first to leave on the bus caravan. I took my four daughters, Shirley, Jenette, Kathleen, and Ida and went on the Mule Train. I had always heard about Washington, D.C., and I really thought that if we went there, maybe our government would help make our lives better. We first had a little trouble getting started, but Andrew Young, Hosea Williams and our wagon master, Rev. Willie Bolden, finally got us started on May 13, 1968.

Mrs. Collins, were you disappointed by your trip to Washington?
Yes and no. I really enjoyed the whole experience, and I learned what we could do if we stuck together. I had never marched like that before. I saw my government turn us down. But the experience lifted my spirits and changed the way I think forever. I got back here, and I don't say "yes suh, boss" anymore. Lots of people around here were real disappointed because they thought things would change right away. But I just trusted in the Lord like I always did, and having been to Washington on the Mule Train, I got a job at Head Start. Worked there for two years and then I went to work at a high school as a cook. Stayed there until I retired.

Today, I have a comfortable home. Most of my children are doing pretty good. A few of them are still here in Mississippi—in Clarksdale and Jackson. They got decent jobs. Three of my girls is up there in Hampton, Virginia, and a bunch of the others is kinda scattered around New York. Jo Lee made a few mistakes. He's in jail in New York. Lula died and Janie's been having a rough time of it up there. I have her son Andre here with me. He's a fine young man. What I like about him, he tries hard. Thank God there be no cotton fields for him. That's all I was hoping for when I went to Washington, was to make things better for my family.

■ ■ ■

INTERVIEW WITH JOAN CASHIN AND MYRNA COPELAND

Joan Cashin, an African-American woman, and Myrna Copeland, a white woman, were politically active in civil rights activities in Huntsville, Alabama. Both participated in the Mule Train and also assisted in mobilizing others. Mrs. Copeland also assembled a group of women, including Mrs. Cashin, to make cloth covers for the wagons. I interviewed Joan Cashin (comments indicated by "JC" in the transcript) and Myrna Copeland ("MC") at the end of the weekend before the Mule Train embarked. We were riding back to Marks after spending a day or so in Huntsville, where we'd gone to rest after a day and a half of rain. The Mule Train's departure had been rescheduled for Monday, May 13. Shortly after we got under way, I recorded a brief addendum with Mrs. Cashin that appears at the end of the interview.

Joan and her husband, John Cashin (see next section for his comments), were politically active in Alabama, both locally in the Huntsville area and statewide. Their lives clearly

instilled strong social concerns in their daughter, Sheryll D. Cashin, an attorney who served on Justice Thurgood Marshall's staff and is currently assistant professor of law at Georgetown University. Joan Cashin passed away in early 1997. Myrna Copeland has remained active in local and state politics in Alabama. She still lives in Huntsville, where she runs a health food store.

* * *

How did you all get involved with the Mule Train?
JC: The Community Service Committee is a local, independent, civil rights activist group. It is incorporated with SCLC and other projects, including Project Vision. Dr. King had visited Huntsville during the sit-ins in 1962. We got involved in helping with the Mule Train because my husband, Dr. John Cashin, chairman of the organization and a dentist from Huntsville, happened to see Hosea Williams in Montgomery about one week before the Mule Train was due to start. Reverend Williams had found it very difficult to locate mules and wagons in the Black Belt of Mississippi and Alabama, so we volunteered to try and locate some. We went back to Huntsville and called around to Tennessee and northern Alabama and located enough for a train of fifteen complete wagons.

In trying to locate mules and wagons, John found that as he began to call around and the word got out, prices went up. Mules went up from $75 to $125, and wagons to between $50 and $100, depending on their condition. Someone decided that they could make some trouble by calling the FBI and telling them anonymously that John was trying to corner the market on mules, and the local FBI began to investigate. Finally, they got the brilliant idea that they should call him directly and just ask what it was all about. And we told them what he was doing and asked what kind of crime that was, and they said it was no crime, they just wanted to know, in case there was any trouble, what was going on.

One of the biggest problems was that we located mules as far away as Arkansas and Kentucky and had the problem of transportation. In one case we had a man who committed himself to taking a truck over to Marks, but when he found out what it was about, he refused to go. And it was very difficult to find cattle cars, and in order to ship the wagons, we had to take them apart and mount them on flatbed trucks. So then the problem was to put them back together in Marks. John and I and Myrna Copeland went down to put the wagons together. Mrs. Copeland had been in charge of getting the material, designing, and making wagon covers. Volunteers who worked on three or four sewing machines for two days did this at her home.

When we got to Marks, we worked for one and a half days putting together the wagons. We found that

Joan Cashin, her daughter Sheryll, and two unidentified local boys are waiting to help waterproof the Mule Train wagon covers.
GRENADA, MISSISSIPPI, MAY 17, 1968 © 1998 JOHN CASHIN

some of them, when delivered, were actually only wheels and the toe and chassis, so we had to build beds for them, and for people to ride, we had to put seats in all the wagons. And then, we had hoops or bowls made in Huntsville which were mounted on each to act as a frame for a cover. When we got to Marks, we had expected to help, especially as my husband had become quite an expert on mules and wagons during the past week. But we didn't realize until we got there that he would end up being the head carpenter. Fortunately, he is talented in carpentry, and he became the man in charge of putting together the wagons and getting them set up. We had the wagons ready on time for the rescheduled departure—the first time we had planned to leave was postponed because the mules were taking a long time to be shod. We had the wagons ready the next day, but the mules were still not ready. So the wagon train, which was due to leave Thursday (May 9) and had been put off until Friday noon, was again put off until Monday noon.

How did it come to pass that your husband was the one chosen for these tasks? I mean, there were others at the meeting with Hosea Williams, why did he take it upon himself to do all this?
JC: Well, my husband was at a meeting of the Civil Rights Commission. It was an open hearing by the National Commission, and he is a member of the State Advisory Committee. The reason that he became the one is because he volunteered, and that's the type of person he is. He saw from the progress that they were making that somebody would have to take some fast action to really get this Mule Train off the ground, and that's the way he operates. If he decides something has to be done, he goes gung-ho, and so he spent most of last week out of his office, calling around finding mules and wagons, and getting them picked up and packed off to Marks.

To give some background on our past activities, we have been deeply involved in civil rights and political actions for over five years now. In 1962, when the sit-in started in Huntsville, our organization, the Community Service Committee, was started to support the sit-in demonstrators, to get them out of jail, to raise money for food and transportation—all the expenses you have with demonstrations, which went on for six months continually. And since then we have been involved in the school desegregation projects. We both work with the Council on Human Relations, and I am secretary-treasurer of the local antipoverty committee and a state board member of the council. My husband is a local board member of the ACLU (American Civil Liberties Union); Mrs. Copeland is the chairman of the north Alabama chapter of the ACLU and secretary of the state board. She's been working with the council and supporting the Community Service Committee all the time it has been in existence.

Having spent a weekend with your family, it set my mind to wondering whether most middle-class Negroes in the South, especially here in the Deep South where you live, are as secure as you all? Would you say that most here have found their place in life in terms of employment and social status, and are concerned with the problems of the less fortunate in the region? Do most of them actively work in these different organizations, or is it just a few who seem to feel this way?
JC: I think it's very unfortunate that it is a minority of the Negro middle class who is actively involved in any type of community action. The largest middle-class group is the teachers, and they, the ones who are most influencing our youth, are the hardest to get involved. And, of course, in a way you can understand this because they are employed by the city or the state and they feel that they can't afford to do too much. But there are others, particularly ministers, who are not tied down, yet who often don't take a chance to do something for poor people of their race. They are satisfied to make it on their own, and they forget about the rest.

Mrs. Copeland, as you're a white citizen of Alabama, I'm particularly interested in some of your perspectives. Are you a native of Alabama? Have you lived here most of your life?
MC: No, I'm not a native Alabamian, but I've lived here all my adult life. I moved here eleven years ago.
Where are you from originally?
MC: New York City.

Oh, I thought I didn't detect as much of that sweet magnolia flowing from your mouth as I would have for a native! Have you encountered many problems since you've become quite active in the Civil Rights movement?
MC: No, not outside of threatening phone calls, and we controlled that by getting an unlisted phone. Also, we weren't able to get a car pool for my kindergarten-aged youngster so we had to take him out of kindergarten. But aside from that—of course my

livelihood doesn't depend on city or state government. I've been working in the poverty program, and my husband works for the federal government, so economically, we are secure and we haven't had the problems that some native Alabamians whose livelihood depends on the goodwill of the population have had. It is very difficult for white citizens like that to do anything openly for civil rights.

Mrs. Copeland, I'd like to ask you about the group of women who helped sew the tops for the wagons. Did you have any trouble getting these people together? Were they already an established committee, or were these a few choice friends who were sympathetic to what was happening? And how did they feel about the idea of taking a group of people from Mississippi by wagon train across a large part of the country, something that I don't think has been done in the last hundred years?
MC: Well, the people that helped on the wagon covers are all very close friends of the Cashins and of my husband and I. We all see the wagon train as a symbol, and one that Dr. King was interested in promoting. It is a symbol of the really poor people of the South, the old mule and the wagon that the very poor dirt farmers of the Old South, both black and white, have been tied to for generations. And they all were very anxious to help. Most of the people that were working on the wagon covers were professors and associate professors at the University of Alabama and the Alabama A&M College in Huntsville, or were professional people.

JC: All white, except one. Of the about ten people who worked on this, all of them were white except Dr. Drake and myself.

Myrna Copeland, Mule Train participant
NEAR BATESVILLE, MISSISSIPPI, MAY 14, 1968

Here's another thing I'd like to ask either of you. I've only been with the SCLC now for about three weeks, and I come from a part of this country where everything seems much more time controlled. Since I've been here, I've noticed that with the various pressures that a lot of folks are feeling, there's been a lot of concern about what some see as a disregard or disrespect for time, especially among the press. Would you comment on how you feel about how the SCLC operates?

MC: Well, as Andy Young says, the Movement is a movement, and a movement shouldn't be forced or expected to meet deadlines. A movement of people is just an upsurge of their opinion and feelings. When you're working with the feelings of people, you can't be expected to meet deadlines and have everything go on schedule.

JC: Well, I think that observers who have not been involved in activity here in the South may think from what they see that it is totally unorganized, real chaos. But I think the SCLC is now better organized than any other national organization in the South, and it seems very typical to me to appear as though a lot of people don't seem to know what to do or what is going on or what would be next. It's a matter of working with what you have, and so whoever volunteers, you work with them. Usually, it is a small hard core of people—whether it is a new group who have just been thrown together as they have been in Marks, or whether it is an established community organization. It takes a few enthusiastic people to light the spark and get it moving. And as you begin to get things together, others will join. Now I think a lot of people felt that the Mule Train would never start at all, and it might not have if we hadn't gotten the mules and wagons. And I think the newspeople still have some doubts about whether it will start and whether it will last, but we never had any doubt that it would. And because a few people don't doubt that it will, we will get to Washington.

Do you feel that the press in this area is giving fair coverage to what is happening? Is it treating it all with other than a traditional southern point of view?

JC: Well, I haven't read too many papers in the last few days, but generally, you don't get a favorable attitude except from a paper like the *Huntsville Times*, sometimes a paper like the *Birmingham News*. The small papers throughout the South usually have, if not an openly segregationist, at least a conservative right-wing attitude toward these things, and it's really hard to tell from them what the general feeling is. I'm sure there is more hostility, more of a feeling that it shouldn't be done, than there is hope that it will be successful.

MC: Well, there is only one newspaper that Mrs. Cashin didn't mention that I thought of, and that's

the *Chattanooga Times*, which is connected, I believe, with the *New York Times*. They usually give favorable or at least fairly objective reporting of civil rights activities in the South. Most other newspapers either ignore, or are discouraging, or are very, very detrimental in their comments. And we feel for the most part that the press in the South has been consistently unfavorable to the Civil Rights movement. For instance, they enjoy mentioning people's names, giving precise information on addresses and where they can be found. I think a lot of harm has come to people who have been active in the Civil Rights Movement because of the kind of coverage that is given. Either they won't say anything at all, or they'll say very little and mention the names of people. Maybe this is the first time this person has ever stood up and said anything, and they'll give it precise coverage to knock them down so they'll never come again.

Do you know specifically of any people who would like to work in some way in the Civil Rights movement, but who, because of this, have declined to do so?

JC: Well, I know there are a lot of people who are put off by this. We have gotten a lot of phone calls, particularly after the Reverand Martin Luther King was killed. We got calls from what we call "nervous liberals," actually outright segregationists, who suddenly felt so much guilt that they had to call and talk to us and say how sorry they were that he was killed. What they really wanted was for us to tell them it was all right, we don't blame you. And I really got sick of it, although they were well-meaning. They never asked what they could do; they never offered to give any money. All they wanted was for us to soothe their guilt. Now that's one category of people.

Then there are other people, white people that I call "do-gooders," who will do certain things in the community, though usually without hitting the hard-core problems. They will gather clothes or food for the poor, or baskets for Christmas, but it's really just paternalism. They're not interested in helping people get jobs, or hiring them so that they wouldn't have to give them food or clothes.

And there is another category of people who are really concerned, but just too timid to come out and get involved. They are afraid for their jobs, or of what their neighbors would think, or what their friends would think. And it can be a pretty lonely life for a white liberal if you don't happen to have a group of friends who agree with you. I know of a few people who have been almost totally ostracized by their old friends. They had to find new ones who feel the same way they do.

Do you think the Poor People's Campaign would have gotten off with the same roaring start if Dr. King hadn't died? I ask this because in the months before his death, national opinion seemed to be going against him, and a lot of people were saying he was really losing his grip. Then immediately after his death, things seemed to change, as if a lot of people thought that since this was one of his last dreams, we had better try to pull it off. Do you think if he had not died we'd be seeing the same spirit that now seems to motivate people within the campaign?

JC: I think the campaign would have gone on and would have been successful. Unfortunately, though, whenever you have a tragedy, that moves people more. I think there is a lot more enthusiasm and determination to really make it successful now than there would have been in the beginning with Reverend King leading it. But I think that toward the end, the pitch of enthusiasm and determination will be about the same whether he was here or not.

One additional comment. I was thinking of comparing this with when Kennedy was killed. A lot of people who couldn't stand him at that time feel now that he was a great president. And of course Johnson was very unpopular until he said he would not run, and now he's more popular and has more personal appeal than he ever had. And it's unfortunate that only now that King has died that people realize he was the greatest hope this country ever had for a nonviolent change in the situation. A revolution, a nonviolent revolution, must go on. But people who cursed him while he was living now revere him, and I hope it's not too late for the people who were dedicated to his cause to carry it on, rather than have the violent elements take over.

Getting back to the Mule Train itself, I'd like to raise this question. The initial plan was to travel all the way from Marks to Washington by mule, and now we've come to realize that this may not be possible. From Marks to Atlanta is almost five hundred miles, and it'll take us about twenty days to get there, which will bring us almost to the date we are due in Washington. So I think we are going to have to do what Andy Young said, travel so far, then put the wagons on flatbeds and the mules on trucks and drive to maybe fifteen or twenty miles outside of Washington, and then go in. How do you feel about something of this sort happening?

JC: I think in order to be kind to the people and the mules, it would be logical to do some shipping, particularly over the mountainous areas like the Appalachian and Blue Ridge that are so difficult to get over, between Georgia and the East Coast. I think that just getting started, getting out of Marks and through Alabama to Georgia, and the symbolism of arriving in Washington will be noticed and announced—even though this may be torn apart by a few newsmen who'll say we really didn't accomplish what we set out to do. I think the effort it took just to get the wagon train together, the people who are willing to take this very hard ride, and the symbolism

of what it really means to have mules instead of Cadillacs—these are the most important things to me, rather than being able to say that the mules walked every mile of the way between Marks and Washington.

As far as the Poor People's Campaign itself is concerned, I'd like to know if you really think that after all these people from the four corners of the United States—the Indians who will come out of Seattle on the train; the Mexican-Americans who will come out of Los Angeles, Denver, and New Mexico; and the caravans that will come out of Boston, Chicago, and the South—descend upon Washington, and we set up these New Cities of Hope that Congress is going to meet any of the demands that Dr. Abernathy took before them two weeks ago?

MC: I don't know. I think it's probably a bad year to ask Congress to respond favorably to a movement like this. There are a number of congressmen, particularly liberals and moderates, who are up for reelection this November, and putting them on the spot like this is going to be very difficult. I don't know if we're going to get any concrete or large-scale action before the next session—the 84th Congress—meets next spring.

Are you saying that you think the likely lack of action is mainly because it's an election year and, for some in Congress, their constituents back home may not be in full agreement with this and that would put them somewhat in trouble?

MC: Yes, definitely. And you see right now that organizations like the Americans for Democratic Action and the Concerned Moderate Citizens of America are desperately trying to gather funds in support of the more liberal congressmen to return them to Washington this fall. And I think a lot of them are in danger of losing their seats. I personally would hate to see them pushed into putting through legislation that would help our Poor People's Campaign if it meant them losing their seats, because in the long run I think we are going to be worse off if we lose the liberal vote that we have in Congress today. I think we also have an obligation to these men who have supported us in the past to keep them in Congress where they can help us in the future.

Well, Mrs. Copeland, bearing this in mind, how do you explain that you are still very active in the Poor People's Campaign?

MC: I wish you hadn't asked that! I think this is something that has to be done. Perhaps this can be looked on as an education for the people of America. I think a lot of Americans just don't realize, are ignorant of how many poor people live in the U.S. I know that a good many of the middle-class white Americans who worked in our poverty program didn't even realize that these people existed before they actually worked with them. They didn't realize the absolute destitution, the dirt and poorness [sic] of the people who were living right in our own county, Madison County, home of the state capital, and the center of the universe in Alabama! I think there are a lot of people in the U.S. that are in that same situation, and until we actually show them the poor, the great numbers of poor people we have in America, they won't be motivated to do something or to back Congress to do something in Washington.

So your convictions are sort of clashing here. On the one hand, you realize what this may do to various members of Congress whom you think are good to have in office, and at the same time you are working for this campaign which may put them in a very touchy situation as far as reelection is concerned. Is that accurate?
MC: Yes, I guess so. But as I said, I think that perhaps the educational benefits of this campaign for the people of America can do more good than harm for the reelection of the more liberal, broad-minded senators and representatives that we have in Washington. So I think in the long run this will be a healthy thing for America. It will be America coming to grips with and facing the reality of what sort of country we really do have, and it should make a lot of people begin to take action, real action. Not just in the voting booth, but it should bring more people out to change the face of America and bring a rapprochement between what America is and what America says it is.

Most of the people I've met who are participating have been recruited here in the South. After all of this is over, they're going to have to come back home. In Marks, I learned of a situation where a plantation owner, after finding out that a woman had been visited by the SCLC field-workers, came the next morning with a shotgun in his hand, kicked open her door, and scared her kids half to death. By the time the SCLC workers got there, he had thrown out all this woman's belongings—which only consisted of a couple of spreads tied with rags—and she was frightened out of her mind. Many of these people are going to Washington because they don't have much to lose, but they are going to have to come back to Tennessee, Alabama, Mississippi, and Georgia to live and stand a real chance of suffering. What do you think is going to happen to these people when they return from Washington?
MC: Well I think the only hope, and this has been true all along the line, the only safety for blacks in the South is unity—and when I speak of unity I mean the middle-class Negro in the South, not just the really poor. There has to be complete unity. If they were all united in working for the betterment of the South, then they wouldn't have to worry about exclusion or fear tactics when they returned here because the white man in the South can't do without the black man. The whole economy here depends on him. If all of them stood together for what was right, then they could force the white man economically. We don't have to worry about changing the heart and the soul of the white man because economically we could force him to do 70 or 80 percent of what is right.

Even in an age of automation, especially throughout the Mississippi Delta, where thousands and thousands of farm workers are constantly being put out of work and becoming completely lost because this is all they know, do you really think this is so?
MC: Have you ever heard of Black Power? If 60 or 70 percent of the population is black, and they're united for civil rights, for making America the land of opportunity, then the white man has no choice but to toe the line. That's what we are talking about when we're talking about the Delta and the Black Belt.

Would you care to comment on that, Mrs. Cashin?
JC: Well, I agree with her. In specific cases there may be a problem for people who are known by name and residence to have gone to Washington. I know the staff discussed this in Marks, and they mentioned that they would leave a staff person there and continue mass meetings. This is one way they are going to try to prevent discrimination after the bulk of the people who are going, leave, including staff. They discussed having someone stay and continue weekly mass meetings to let the people downtown know there is someone watching and that the people are still together.

Do you really think this will help prevent harassment or intimidation?
JC: Well, it won't stop it, but it'll probably serve as notice that they can't really run over them completely. Being in this kind of thing, you have to have the attitude that Dr. King had. If you once make the decision that you are going to be in it up to your neck, you can't worry about what's going to happen, because if you do, then you are totally useless in any strategy you plan. So we just decided to move out several years and we don't look back. And you have to maintain your own peace of mind and just not worry about it. Now I admit that some of these poor people who have not been involved may be meeting intimidation for the first time, and it may be frightening to them. But I think if we worry about, say, preventing people from being frightened, what we are really saying is let's not rock the boat, let's not shake up the system. It has to be done, and there is no doubt there will be sacrifices because of it.

Well, tell me this. Most of the poor people who have been recruited here, do you think they have a full awareness of what the Poor People's Campaign is all about or how vast it is in scope? Do you think this is important, or is it enough for them to know that they are poor and that someone is taking them to Washington to present their case to Congress to help them seek a better way of life? Do you think they are well enough informed?

JC: I think they are because they know what the problems are. They may not be able to explain the philosophical nature of passive resistance, but they certainly know that they don't have what they need, and that it's about time to demand it. I think that among the people I've talked with, there's no doubt that they are very much determined to do whatever they can to cooperate, and I think grassroots people quite often can articulate their problems and what they need much better than social scientists. Although they may not be able to say it well enough to be on TV and explain it as well as Andy Young did on the *Today Show*, I think they are very intelligent people—they have to be just to survive.

Would you like to comment on this, Mrs. Copeland?

MC: I think Mrs. Cashin is right. What we as middle-class Americans might think is ignorance on the part of the black people in the Deep South that are taking part in this campaign, might actually be our sense that they are rather ignorant about the philosophy behind the movement. But when it comes down to the nitty-gritty of what this campaign is all about, they know more about it than we do because they've lived through the destitution and the poverty that has caused a movement like this, and when they're put up against the wall, they can tell you why they are going to Washington and can tell it in a much more sorrowful way than we could.

This addendum to the interview was recorded on May 13, 1968, shortly after the Mule Train had left Marks. Mrs. Cashin had been riding in one of the lead wagons when the mules broke away for a moment and she fell off. She was one of the first persons to get hurt, though not very seriously.

Mrs. Cashin, would you like to comment on this traumatic experience that you just had?

JC: Well, all I have to say is it was my fault. I didn't really fall off. Rather, the mules were running away, and though the driver stopped them eventually, I was trying to calculate whether they would go over the ditch on the side of the road. I knew I would be pushed off if they did. So, when the driver jumped down between the mules to stop them, I decided I'd better get off. But I didn't realize how fast the wagon was moving, so when I jumped off I caught my foot.

■ ■ ■

COMMENTS BY JOHN CASHIN

As indicated in the preceding interview with his wife, Joan, Dr. John Cashin was deeply involved in the Civil Rights movement and quite active in both local and statewide politics in Alabama. For the Mule Train, he was instrumental in locating and preparing the mules and wagons needed. Now retired from his dentistry practice, Dr. Cashin continued his activism after the Poor People's Campaign, which included a run for governor of Alabama. On February 9, 1998, after we'd had several conversations and he'd reviewed the transcript of Mrs. Cashin's interview, he provided the following written comments in response to the indicated questions.

* * *

When did you first hear about the Mule Train, and what was your initial reaction?

Dr. Randolph Blackwell and I had discussed the dramatic effect of a Mule Train in 1962 when we used a mule in our voter registration drive in Huntsville. Our mule carried a sign, "I can't vote because I'm a mule—what's your excuse?" It was a very effective ploy, and we thought about someday using a mule train on national TV to call attention to the "forty acres and a mule" that we didn't get during Reconstruction!

I had filed a charter and by-laws for our own political party, the National Democratic Party of Alabama (NDPA), on 15 December 1967, and Dr. King, Dr. Randolph T. Blackwell, and I had spent many hours on the phone discussing the most effective way to harness the electoral power of the semi-literate voters recently franchised by the Voting Rights Act of 1965. "Even a mule can mark an 'X'" almost became our slogan! Our phone conversations were obviously tapped by the FBI and company. The Supreme Court ruled NDPA on the Alabama ballot the last week in March 1968, and King was killed the very next week, on April 4, 1968.

(*left to right*) John Cashin, his daughter Sheryll Cashin and Joan Cashin (1936-1997) at Sheryll's home

Would you expand on what's already in the interview with Mrs. Cashin as to how you initially got involved in the Mule Train, how you ended up in a leadership position, and why you believed it was important?

To comprehend my role with the Mule Train, you must know first about Alabama in 1962. The state was totally segregated as a direct result of the white supremacy Alabama Constitutional Convention of 1901. As power tends to corrupt and as absolute power corrupts absolutely, the Alabama Constitution of 1901 gave white males total control of everything in Alabama via five subterfuges designed to circumvent the United States Constitution in general, and its 13th, 14th, and 15th amendments in particular. The arrogance of absolute power had spawned a number of laws drawn up by the 100 percent white male Alabama Legislature, including one sponsored by John Patterson in 1956 which made it a crime, punishable by a $1,000.00 fine and up to one year in prison, just to be a member of the NAACP or CORE!

When the sit-in movement began in Huntsville on 3 January 1962, black Huntsville organized itself to meet the challenge. We started our own ad hoc civil rights organization, the Community Service Committee (CSC). I was its Vice-Chairman. Huntsville had the most successful of all the sit-in campaigns nationwide, and we did it without violence or bloodshed. This is probably why our campaign was relatively obscure. The news media generally pays attention only to the very worst in America.

Anyway, we were very well organized, and had almost 100 percent support of the Huntsville black population. There also were a significant number of progressive whites, especially from the Unitarian and Episcopal Churches, who marched along with us as real brothers and sisters. We were so successful that we looked for other areas where our experience would be needed. Dr. Blackwell, a key member of our leadership committee, was recruited by Dr. King to help organize SCLC. He was a graduate of the Howard University School of Law, as well as a disciple of A. Phillip Randolph. This connection pretty much made the Huntsville CSC a branch of the SCLC. We did everything we could to support Randy Blackwell, for he was "family."

In 1964 Sam Simmons and Carl Holman recruited me as a member of the Alabama Advisory Committee to the U.S. Commission on Civil Rights. In late April, a few weeks after Dr. King was assassinated, the Commission held its first public hearing in ten years, in Montgomery. Hosea Williams was our last witness on Thursday evening. He asked if anybody could give SCLC some help with the Mule Train. They had announced in a press release that they were going to pull out the following Tuesday with 125 wagons and 600 mules, and they had only been able to locate two wagons and six mules.

I called Reverend Blackwell and he verified the predicament. I told him to postpone the Marks departure for two weeks, and I would find enough mules and wagons to keep SCLC from being embarrassed. They had been looking in the wrong places. Middle Tennessee and northeast Alabama had enough hills that tractors couldn't plow, and Columbia, Tennessee, was known as the "mule capital of the world." I called my bail bondsman, Albert Lee Kelley, and my Omega[23] brother, Warren Q. Scott, who was Alabama A&M's Agricultural Extension Agent, and told them to get busy. By the time I got back to Huntsville on Sunday, they had located almost 60 mules and perhaps 25 wagons, all in "as is" states of repair.

So, I was involved in the Mule Train from its inception in conversations with King and Blackwell. I ended up in a leadership position because there was no one else who understood the big picture, and I knew it was important because I had promised King that I would do it if anything happened to him. Keeping your word to a dead compatriot is an extremely important duty in my culture!

Describe the direct involvement you maintained once the Mule Train got under way.

One continuing involvement was in the wording of the messages that were painted on the sides of the wagons. "Stop the War, Feed the Poor" and "Jesus Was a Marcher Too" were two of my favorites. These messages were seen five or six times daily on national TV, which was the main idea of the Mule Train in the first place. It really attracted attention when the state of Georgia said we could not use the interstate highway system. When we got on the interstate anyway, the TV cameras spread the news worldwide, as Blackwell and I had predicted.

Another involvement was on the second or third day out of Marks, after a rainstorm had showed that the thin muslin covers, great for sign painting, did not shelter the occupants adequately. So the Huntsville support team met them in Mississippi, Clarksdale or Grenada, I think, and recovered the wagon bows with 5-millimeter plastic sheeting. They then put the original covers—with their all-important signs—back over the plastic. This provided sufficient water-proofing for the rest of the journey.

Would you like to add comments to any parts of the interview with Mrs. Cashin?

Only that she, Myrna (Copeland), and the "dreck set" answered the call with heroic performances. Our Huntsville "dreck set"—derived from a Yiddish word—was an avant-garde, genuinely integrated group, which essentially was the executive leadership of the National Democratic Party of Alabama. We also led the Alabama challenge delegation to the August

[23] Omega Psi Phi, one of America's three major black fraternities.

1968 Democratic National Convention in Chicago. But that's another story!

What impact did the experience have on you and Mrs. Cashin?
It brought us closer together and prepared us as a family for even greater challenges to come. And since Ralph Abernathy, Hosea Williams, Andy Young, and Joe Lowery never saw fit to reimburse me for the over $27,000 I had expended on SCLCs behalf, it taught us to be very wary of preachers and their promises!

In general, what impacts do you think the Mule Train had on the poor people from Mississippi, Alabama, and Georgia who participated in it?
It gave inspiration and courage to those who had been demoralized by King's murder and dramatized the fact that, if any changes were going to take place, we must force the issues ourselves.

What impact do you think it had on middle-class blacks from those same areas—especially on those who had previously been relatively inactive in the movement?
Little or none. Mostly a conversation piece.

What, if any, impact do you think the Poor People's Campaign had on the ongoing civil rights or social justice agendas?
Major impact! The highlight of the Democratic National Convention in Chicago was Fannie Lou Hamer and Willie Brown speaking for the Alabama NDPA challenge. It even moved Richard Nixon to create an Office of Minority Business Enterprise. The idea of poor people voting intelligently changed a lot of things.

What are your most vivid memories of your own experience with the Poor People's Campaign?
Of an honors graduate of Meharry Medical College (me!) shoeing mules in the Mississippi mud! Wow! Of seeing our primitive wagons and their messages on network TV. Of Andy Young leading mules down the wagon path. Of my wife almost being raped in Resurrection City. Of SCLC not refunding the money I spent on their behalf. Of courageous true believers undertaking an historic journey.

How would you sum up in one sentence why this event is important to remember?
"As you have done it to the least of these, you have done it to me."

∎ ∎ ∎

INTERVIEW WITH WILLIE BOLDEN

Rev. Willie Bolden was an SCLC staff member from Atlanta. He was selected by the SCLC to be the wagon master for the Mule Train and, as such, had overall responsibility for its successful completion of the voyage from Marks to Washington. Reverend Bolden currently works for the Atlanta Board of Education as coordinator for the Department of Employee Relations. He is also pastor of a rural church outside Atlanta. I interviewed him over the phone on February 28, 1998, following several preliminary conversations about his memories of the Mule Train.

* * *

How did you first get involved with the Mule Train?
It was first discussed at the SCLC headquarters in Atlanta. I was a staff member, and along with others, I was assigned to go to Marks, Mississippi, and organize for it.

Leading up to the time that the Mule Train left Marks, there were a lot of setbacks. What role did this play in the undertaking?
At first there was the problem of getting enough mules and decent wagons; but John Cashin, out of Alabama, was really helpful with this. We had been organizing all around Quitman County and some of the adjoining counties. R. B. Cottonreader and I had both been locked up for just talking to people—those Mississippi sheriffs were some nasty people. Then just dealing with the logistics of where to put all the folks who were showing up to go on the Mule Train was a real challenge. We had to erect some big tents just so that folks would have some place to sleep, out of the rain.

I had a lot of help from SCLCs veteran field-workers. James Bevel was helping to register people for the Poor People's Campaign. He was not only trying to get people to go on the Mule Train, but on the buses that were part of the southern caravan that was to leave Marks for Resurrection City, in Washington. Andrew Marrsett, who was out of Birmingham (AL), was also there helping to organize. Then there were Andy Young and Hosea Williams who came in to help spearhead all of these efforts. Right after King was killed we had more volunteers than we knew what to do with; everybody wanted to help. You know Andy was always our diplomat, the soft-spoken, cool-headed one, and he was always good with the press. Hosea was the old warhorse; I love him; he's the one that brought me into the movement.

I remember a late-night meeting with SCLC staff when I first got to Marks. You and Andy were discussing how important it was to teach these new folks the freedom songs. Can you expand on this?
Since the Mule Train was one of Dr. King's last wishes, SCLC assembled some of their best senior field-workers in Marks, as I have said before. With this wonderful team assembled, we decided that it was necessary at all of the workshops to teach all

these new folks the freedom songs, along with nonviolent tactics. Songs and prayers were staples of the movement. They gave you courage, so when we held mass rallies and workshops, we taught the people the freedom songs. In most cases, these songs were new lyrics added to old church songs that most people already knew. Local folks really loved it; it seemed like everybody turned out for these meetings. People were fired up, and we were trying to give them proper direction.

One of our biggest headaches was that the weather wasn't good. We used to just sit down late in the evening and talk about what life must have been like for the pioneers going out West, and how they traveled in mule trains in similar situations. I mean, I know that for us it was raining and cold, and in almost every town that we went into we didn't sleep in hotels. Some people slept on the wagons, some slept in homes, and others slept in churches. Some people stayed up all night and didn't sleep at all. Most of the time, I took catnaps. I felt responsible for seeing that everybody got a place to sleep, but it was tough. Like I said before, the weather was really bad, but I don't remember anybody ever really complaining about the conditions we had to cope with while we made that journey. I know that it wasn't the best of situations, but we made do.

Wagon Master Willie Bolden
TUSCALOOSA, ALABAMA, MAY 28, 1968

Why do you think people were so motivated?
I think that it was because of unity and commitment, and that we got folks to understand that this was not going to be an easy journey. It had never been done before. We didn't know of anyone in our time that had undertaken such a task. We were going to have to stick together. In the morning, I would give pep talks, and I would preach in the evenings at mass rallies. I would solicit help from the local communities at these meetings. We were received well in almost every community that we stopped in. They were poor folks just like us.

Aside from the people that you have mentioned, do you recall any of the other people that you worked with on the Mule Train?
As I said before, I was working with Andy Young, Hosea Williams, James Bevel, R. B. Cottonreader, Andrew Marrsett, as well as other guys who were working together to organize the community for the Poor People's Campaign.

Today when people talk about the Civil Rights movement, they usually mention the names of men. When I think back on the Mule Train, I also remember a lot of hardworking women, wonderful sisters who kept everything going. They were very serious and seemed never to miss a beat. So, now that people are writing about the history of this period, we must never forget the courageous sisters who laid their lives on the line for the struggle.
You're absolutely right. I remember that my right-hand person was a woman named Margorie Hyatt—I think she was from Pittsburgh. Everybody used to call her Margie. She was the one who kept all the records for me, a count of all of the feed that we needed for the mules, like hay and oats. She made sure we would always have enough. I would get a report on this daily. I wanted to make sure that everything was done right because we knew that the authorities were watching us. I was sure that the authorities and the newspapers would have loved to report that we were mistreating the mules. So, every day before we pulled out in the morning, I would check with the muleskinners to make sure that all the mules had sufficient horseshoes and that they were fed, rubbed down, and taken care of. We also had to make sure that we had enough to eat. I had a number of people helping me with these logistics and keeping up with the equipment. Margie was always there to remind me if I forgot anything.

There was another woman name Faye Porche, who handled finance for SCLC. She made sure that we had receipts for everything. There was also Bertha Johnson (Luster) from Marks who first worked at SCLCs Marks headquarters. Even though she had five or six children with her on the Mule Train, she was still always busy helping other people. As I can remember, there was a whole team of hardworking women, though I can't remember them all.

Who was the brother who did the cooking at the rest stops?
That was Lester Hankerson from Savannah, Georgia.

Tell me, what were some of the most memorable events that took place on the way?
There were several memorable experiences enroute to Washington, two of which stand out in my mind right now. The first was when we got to Georgia and had the confrontation with the governor there, Lester Maddox. We had come across Mississippi and Alabama, and the governors of both these states had protected us. They had the highway patrol block off the streets and roads, whenever necessary. They also allowed us to travel down the interstate. But when we got to Tallapoosa, Georgia, right there at the Alabama line, Governor Maddox and his state patrolmen stopped us and told us we would not be able to continue down I-20. Of course we were determined to do it anyway.

What were the specifics surrounding the confrontation in Tallapoosa?
Well, it all started when the governor had his state troopers take me to his car. They said that the governor wanted to talk to me. The essence of it all was that he was trying to convince me to let him put the mules and wagons on trucks provided by the National Guard, and bus the Mule Train people down Interstate 20 to Atlanta. I think he was afraid that the dramatic appeal of the Mule Train might stir folks up, but I told him, no, we were not going to do that. We hadn't done it in Mississippi or Alabama, and we weren't going to do it in Georgia. So, we were going down I-20, and of course, the governor insisted that we weren't supposed to take that route, and we insisted that we were. Finally, I just got out of the car, slammed the door, and started back toward my folks. That's when he told the troopers to grab me, and they locked some of us up. They didn't keep us too long, maybe four or five hours. It was then that I saw a unity among the Mule Train people there that I will always remember. When they locked some of us up after I insisted that we be allowed to go down I-20, the remaining people, who were on the Mule Train, helped organize with the folks in Tallapoosa. Lester Maddox, fearing that he was about to stir up a hornet's nest, decided that it was better to turn us loose. When they did, we continued down I-20. That was a high point, the unity that I saw the Mule Train people display.

The other experience that I most remember had to be when we got to Washington, and we went across that bridge from Virginia to Washington. Just think of all the caravans that came to Washington that summer, I don't think any of those journeys were as difficult as that of the Mule Train. I prayed hard every night for God to help us carry out one of Dr. King's last wishes: to bring a Mule Train of poor folks from Marks, Mississippi to Washington, D.C. If these people never accomplished anything else in their lives, they accomplished this.

As I understand it, the governors of Mississippi and Alabama had state troopers usher the Mule Train to make sure that it was properly protected. Given what happened in Georgia and that you didn't have the same protection there, do you think that this service made a difference in the Mule Train journey?
I would suspect that having the state troopers there made a difference, if for no other reason than it would have taken us a lot longer to get there if we would have had the kinds of confrontations in Alabama and in Mississippi that we had in Georgia. But I think that by that time in the Civil Rights movement, the governors of Alabama and Mississippi understood that once the SCLC made up its mind to conduct a campaign, it was going to take place one way or another. They keenly remembered the Birmingham struggle and the Selma to Montgomery March, especially the crossing of the Edmund Pettus Bridge at Selma, where mounted police rode people down with cattle prods. Alabamians ended up looking like the worst racists in the eyes of the world because these confrontations were televised on the news, all over the world. So Governor George Wallace and his boys jumping on us resulted in an ever more heightened sympathy for the Civil Rights struggle. I'm sure that this came to their minds, and as a result, their objective was to get us through their states as soon as possible, with no incidents.

Were there any particular strategies that you, as wagon master, had for dealing with the state troopers?
Cooperation. Each day, as near as I could figure it, I'd let them know where we planned to start and what our destination was. Often they would get frustrated because we couldn't start on time, and when we got to where we were going that evening, they would disappear and pick us back up the next morning. Also, there were always these plainclothes people around who I thought were FBI agents.

Aside from the confrontation with Governor Maddox, do any other confrontations stand out in your mind?
No more than a daily harassment by whites. In between rest stops they would drive by blowing their horns, purposely trying to spook the mules and us. On several occasions, especially in the beginning, mules ran off the road and a few people got hurt, but not badly. You have to remember that these were farm mules and it took them a while to get used to the

road. It's just that the confrontation with Maddox made me angry. We had crossed Mississippi and Alabama and Governor Maddox was telling me that here, in my home state, and in the home state of Dr. King, that we couldn't go down I-20.

What do you think about the press coverage you got as you went across the country?
Like all of these campaigns, you get a lot of press coverage in the beginning, and then, unless something dramatic is happening, they lose interest. When this Mule Train started in Marks, the press was everywhere; but after a few days they were almost all gone except for this white woman with NBC, named Jean Smith [Freas],[24] who stayed with us longer than anybody. Of course, there was a lot more press coverage in Washington when we first got there. When I think of it now, I doubt that the incident at the Georgia state line would have even happened if the press had been there.

Looking back, do you think that the expectations of the Mule Train people from Marks were met, and what do you think happened to those expectations once they got to Washington?
Well, as I recall, I don't think they lost hope. I think what happened was that once we got there, and as you may remember, the weather was terrible, there were thousands of people. When we crossed the bridge from Virginia into Washington, I think that there was still a lot of hope, enthusiasm, and motivation. But when we got to Resurrection City, with all the turmoil going on with the shanties and the confrontations with the Washington police, it was just a bit much for these simple folks to handle. The truth of the matter was that we really hadn't gotten a lot of direction from senior SCLC staff. People just kind of got scattered, where before we had been together for some forty to fifty days, traveling down the highway through Mississippi, Alabama, and Georgia. Then, all of a sudden, when we got to our destination, people just got scattered.

Things in Washington began to deteriorate from lack of proper planning. When we got off the train, they bused us to a center outside of the city. But the Mule Train folks had lots of relatives and neighbors who were already in Resurrection City, who had come earlier on the buses that were part of the southern caravan. Of course, the Mule Train folks from Marks wanted to be in Resurrection City with them, so with little direction, some people just left the center and went to stay in Resurrection City with friends and family. I remember we just kind of merged in with everybody else who was there.

[25] See comments from Ms. Freas on next page.

People just got lost, and I think that a lot of frustration set in. That's what I think really happened. Resurrection City was one big chaotic situation, and it was hard to keep up with what was going on. It certainly wasn't as well organized as the March on Washington, or the Mule Train as far as that goes. These people came together and they stayed together, but in Resurrection City, and especially the day we were teargassed, people just got separated.

How did the Mule Train people get back to Mississippi, Alabama, and Georgia, and who made the arrangements?
Many of those people who went back, if my memory serves me correctly, went back on buses with tickets provided by SCLC. Some of them caught rides with other people, and I'm not sure if any flew back.

Did the SCLC ever do any follow-up with the Mule Train or any of its participants that you know of?
To the best of my knowledge, no. I know I certainly did not follow up. As a matter of fact I think it was quite some time before I went back to Marks. I did go back on a couple of occasions, but I don't know of any organized follow-up that ever took place.

What did you do after that summer?
Well, I definitely took some time off! The stress of being responsible for the Mule Train really took a lot out of me. After I recuperated, I returned to my job at SCLC and was assigned to do organizing in Pike County, Georgia. They were trying to fire this black principal from one of the schools there, and so SCLC had a movement going on to protest this.

When did you finally leave the SCLC?
I left SCLC in 1970. Bernard Lafayette, whom I had worked with during the movement and who used to work for the SCLC headquarters in Washington, was working on this doctorate in education at Harvard at that time. He helped me to get a scholarship there, and in a year and a half, I got my master's in education.

Given all that you went through with the Mule Train, how would you convey what happened on it to today's generation?
I think the Poor People's Campaign played a significant role in helping to shape some of the policies that relate to housing and jobs. That was a part of what Resurrection City and the Poor People's Campaign were all about in the first place. By that time we already had the rights granted by the Voters Right Act and the Civil Rights Act, so the Poor People's Campaign was, in my opinion, geared toward housing, jobs, and the distribution of wealth. Certainly I feel that black people are doing a lot better

today than they were then. They certainly hold a lot more positions in corporations across America today. In 1968, this would have been unthinkable. Back then, if anyone had told us that Mr. Chenault would be the head of American Express, and is being groomed now to take over whenever the other guy leaves, you wouldn't have believed that. If anybody had said that Colin Powell would have been selected as Chairman of the Joint Chiefs of Staff, we certainly would not have believed that either. But even now, with all the improvement and gains that we've made, we still have a long way to go.

For the people who came off the plantations of the Mississippi Delta and the Black Belt of Alabama, do you think that the expectations they had when they joined the Mule Train remained, in terms of the promises that had been made?

I'd probably need to go back to see for myself because I'm not sure a lot of promises were made. I think that what was said when we went out recruiting across the United States was that we needed to go to Washington, to the seat of power, to say that we wanted a decent education for our children, and a fair opportunity to work and to better our conditions. You have to remember, back then, Marks was considered if not the poorest place in the United States, very close to it, and very little was done to change this, especially for black folk. I'm sure that Marks looks better today and that a lot of its health and social conditions have gotten better. But on a national scale, it still rates pretty low. I'm sure that many people are still hurting.

■ ■ ■

COMMENTS BY JEAN SMITH FREAS

In the spring of 1968, Jean Smith (now Freas) was a reporter covering the Mule Train for WRC, the NBC television affiliate in Washington, D.C. Mrs. Freas, who is white, was one of very few women covering the Mule Train. She earned the respect and friendship of many of those involved as she stayed with it longer than any other reporter. After the Poor People's Campaign, she continued with WRC until the end of 1969 and then moved to Pennsylvania to devote more time to raising her children while working on a book and covering occasional assignments for NBC. Now retired, Mrs. Freas lives in New York and continues to write. I located her in late 1997 and asked that she send me her reflections about the Mule Train. She prepared the following.

* * *

When the fanfare was over, the Mule Train was ready at last. Mules, some on their last legs, drew the ancient, creaky wagons, which were draped in worn

Jean Smith Freas, a television journalist who provided longer continuous coverage of the mule train than any other reporter

MARKS, MISSISSIPPI, EARLY MAY 1968

canvas. Reminiscent of the popular television show of the sixties, each wagon was commanded by a big man with a whip. About forty women and children of all ages waited quietly. After days of speechifying and picture-taking, these were the volunteers who would actually make that slow, teasing, lurching, tortuous ride along lonely roads to Washington, a temptation sure to excite every bigot and nut case for miles around. I couldn't read the expressions of the men in uniform who made up the sheriff's escort without a question mark; "grim" was one word, "professional," another. The passengers were something else. Bewildered, or scared, a few were stone-faced. After tearful hugs and last-minute huddles with loved ones left behind, the volunteers climbed aboard. Freedom songs rose from the jubilant crowd gathered for the send-off. They knew that ahead, trustworthy people would be waiting. At nightfall, churches twenty miles up the road would provide food and shelter. But right now, and for days after, and after that every few days, the Mule Train did not move, and nobody could tell me why. For the past forty-eight hours, journalists flocking in from all over the globe almost outnumbered the local people, some of whom had fled in fear. Dr. King himself had selected Marks and the Mule Train as the vanguard of what he called the Poor People's Campaign. But once the media acquitted themselves, the world's attention was moving on, and that gave us the exclusive nonstory of whatever came next.

Before joining NBC, I had reported to East Africa for the Voice of America in English and sometimes in Swahili, which I picked up in graduate school. Years earlier, I lived for a time in Oxford, Mississippi. The Emmett Till case was in the news. For the first time I encountered a peculiar local deafness whenever the word "lynching" was mentioned. Perhaps this motley background was my point of departure in covering the Mule Train.

My job was to tell a story, night after night, same characters, same locale, something television news almost never does. Reporting a fire is easier. But eventually our Mule Train coverage won the Associated Press award for televised in-depth reporting.

Coverage which today would cost a small fortune, we did with one reporter, myself, doubling as field producer, with a freelance camera crew from Memphis, led by Bill McAfee, doubling as film courier; union rules meant nothing where we were. Every day we "enterprised" and shot a story, and then raced it to the nearest airport, in time to meet the film editor who would feverishly cut it for the seven o'clock news. We were already nosing around for the next day. Around midnight we turned in somewhere cheap, not the upscale motels favored by the SCLC. To appease the bookkeepers, we had to cut corners.

I conferred daily with my news director. His purpose in sending a local reporter to cover a network story was to show Washington viewers the Mule Train people, a handful among the anonymous hundreds of thousands who would soon converge on the nation's capital. Give the flavor, the lives in brief. And so we did, hoping this was the way to erode some of the mounting ill will and apprehension in our community.

This was a time when a newswoman was a rarity, neither welcomed nor trusted, whether within the movement's macho element, or by the man or woman in the streets, or by patronizing newsmen, as many were.

Bad memories. Pickup trucks, rifles in plain view, sped at me, swerving at the last minute, in time to ruin our shot and send me flying. Entering a café makes people get up and leave. Phone calls and catcalls. Women in white gloves who actually spit. Which was nothing, compared to the tight spots the volunteers could find themselves in. At the very least, theirs was the worst of two worlds, camping out or in an institution, like a jail or a hospital. Though a clutch of federal marshals, even a CIA agent (yes, that's right), stood by in dense woods, don't think for a moment anyone was here to protect you.

Why did these people do it? I found Mrs. Lee Dora Collins, mother of thirteen. Grave demeanor, a deeply religious woman, prayerfully aware of the movement, whose world up to then was Mississippi. The Mule Train was her once-in-a-lifetime chance to make a contribution, perils and all.

As it worked out, volunteers were only part of the story. We met people in this tense community we would never have imagined. The white woman at the grocery store, who took bread to the Mule Train. The deacon whose cheeks trembled with fear. The teenage gospel singer with the glorious voice. A mother caring for her paralyzed son, victim of a gunfight long past. The blind ninety-year-old, in a windowless shack, papered over with newsprint of Dr. King and President Kennedy. The feisty midwife on Lewis Street, who'd brought two hundred babies into the world. All these people, eager to share their story, even though they would never see themselves on television!

What good came from the Mule Train? Look no farther than Locust Street. Thirty years ago, the sick and needy in Marks had no real health care. Then a young nun in Washington, scrubbing clothes for the Mule Train, thought she knew a better use for her talents than teaching high school science. The bishop agreed with her. In due time she became known as Dr. Marilyn Aiello, of the De Porres Delta Health Ministries.

Mrs. Collins, as far as I know, is the only one from the Mule Train still in Marks, so now let's acknowledge her!

A PERSONAL AFTERWORD

REVISITING THE MULE TRAIN

I knew from the excitement I felt last September after talking to Bertha Johnson Luster that developing this book would be an emotional journey. I anticipated neither how emotional nor how important it would become to try to get it right. I realized that at the bottom of why the Mule Train meant so much and its celebration was so important to me lay two elements. The first is the magnificent courage and hope showed by its participants, just ordinary poor people from Marks and elsewhere in the South; the second is the powerful and richly reverberating role it played for me as a rite of passage.

First, for a relatively new photographer, the Mule Train provided a rare opportunity to practice my craft, to learn and deliver under pressure, to be accountable as part of a large and committed team as well as to my own very demanding self. I learned how to handle a significant assignment that extended over time. I had to shoot a lot of film, keeping it focused on the story at hand while also probing deeper into what was going on. I needed to produce continuously and on time. If I didn't get what we needed, that part of the history of the Poor People's Campaign might have been lost.

I learned about maintaining control over my work as I saw a lot of what I and others shot disappear, somewhere between the field and campaign headquarters. I also learned the importance of having duplicate copies of research records, caption material, and personal impressions since many of these were also lost. Finally, I had access to other photographers assigned to the Mule Train—some quite briefly, some for days, some who knew far more about photojournalism than I did. I learned from them, and I grew tremendously.

Also, harking back to the advice given me by my mentor Burke Uzzle, I had engaged, big time, my fear of working in the South, and I had matured as a result. I learned that the South was indeed a place of hard times, and that it justified my fears of arbitrary oppression. But I also learned that it was where there was important work for me to do, alongside solid, talented, and purposeful black folks whose history, skills, and continuing struggle I needed to learn, document, and tell.

Dr. King's death crystallized my decision to focus my professional life on contributing to what I now recognized as a broad, ongoing movement. For me, it meant trying to make sense of the continuity of the lives and cultural expression of black people, of what it means to be black and poor in America, and of the strengths and contributions that they and other groups have brought to the American mosaic. Over my extended assignment with the Mule Train, I was exposed to an exciting combination of organizing, teaching, learning, planning, and reacting. By the time it ended, I understood far more about myself, the world, and how we affect one another.

The experiences of that summer gave voice to my appreciation and understanding of poor people. I was, and certainly had always felt myself, one with them. My relatives in South Carolina and Pennsylvania lived in situations that differed from those of the Mule Train participants only in locale. I had lived anything but a sheltered life. Growing up on the poor streets of Baltimore, working on "arabbing" wagons, and living among sharecroppers in rural southern Maryland, I learned to hustle and hung out with better hustlers than myself, both there and while in Europe in the armed forces. In general, those who passed through my mother's and grandmothers' houses, as well as those with whom I interacted outside their homes, were poor and all too often hungry——though we saw this as a statement of fact about material possessions and limited life choices and not a value judgment. I'm sure this was part of why I enjoyed being among the Mule Train people and meeting those who all along the journey rushed out to greet us. It also helped me understand, and at times be overwhelmed by, the meaning of their contributions to the cause of twenty-five cents or a couple of peanut butter and jelly sandwiches. I wanted my own life to be different, but I certainly knew that I, too, was black and poor, and I wasn't naive about the implications.

During the couple of years prior to the Poor People's Campaign, I had become familiar with the photography of Roy DeCarava, Gordon Parks, and Eugene Smith. I saw that the lives of poor people could be documented with their pride and dignity intact and communicated as a key part of the story being told—and I knew that was what I would demand of my own work. And now, I had the opportunity to test that stance by documenting the sustained strength, courage, and commitment of the Mule Train people during a most difficult time. These poor, often hungry, generally unschooled folks had led hard lives full of risk and uncertainty. And here they were again, never having the whole picture of what was going on; being told to be here or there, to hurry up and wait. They were put on display and regularly placed in potentially confrontational and violent settings. They continuously heard rumors about leadership screwing up, holding back, or selling out.

Through it all, the Mule Train people understood that they ultimately had to put their bodies—and often their lives—on the line. They needed to leave home for an indefinite time, to undergo the stress and rigors of the journey and their living conditions in D.C., to speak out publicly about who they were and how they lived. And then, individually, they had to return home to the same settings they'd left or to start new lives in new places—often to face added hostility from employers and local political structures that looked unkindly at their participation in the campaign.

I learned how to photograph the people of the Mule Train; I learned how, while showing the reality of their lives, to show the strength of their souls, the success of their struggles, and the value to the rest of us of what they preserve and bring to the table. The Mule Train was vital in my learning how to transform personal experience into a continuing partnership with the people who are the subjects of my life work. As my career continued, I realized that it was also an important step in my learning how to portray positively the many aspects of the lives of poor people—how I might provide images fundamentally different from what we usually encounter in American media.

THE BIGGER PICTURE: WHAT DIFFERENCE DID THE POOR PEOPLE'S CAMPAIGN MAKE?

Throughout the development of this book, I could not escape the irony of trying to transform, through sequence and intent, an experience that for me, and most others involved, was best characterized as chaos and confusion. I am amazed at how much, in hindsight, seems to fit and hold together, appears to have been planned, and if not reasonable, is at least understandable. Perhaps that emergence of clarity is an appropriate metaphor for this section.

The Poor People's Campaign, like most large social movements, relied on the willing participation and close collaboration of many groups and individuals. They operated under dispersed, coordinated leadership who brought nuanced, if not contradictory, understandings and substantial egos to goals, strategies, roles, and relationships. And the leader who could have most effectively harmonized the differences and managed the messages, Dr. King, was suddenly ripped from his key role in the midst of final planning. Though this was just a matter of days

before its scheduled start, the campaign was delayed only minimally, and the remaining leaders tried to sort things out as they went along. Once it was under way, it virtually always seemed as if everybody—participants, leaders, media, and protest targets—had different, shifting, and contradictory takes on what was going on and why. If we weren't wrong, we were certainly confused and were seeing only part of the picture.

Now though, over time and with reflection on the broader context, the meaning of the Mule Train and the Poor People's Campaign seems clearer, and to me, its success and importance unarguable. It irreversibly changed the terms of reference and the agenda for change in the United States by incorporating, and then making inseparable, the economic and political dimensions of poverty in America. It also manifested the requirement that the ongoing struggle reach across racial and ethnic lines, and provided an arena to accelerate the process of coalition building. Unfortunately, it also demonstrated the fragility of that process, the amount of prior history and residue that would need to be overcome, the irregular progress that would be made, and the temporal and shifting nature of such alliances.

The campaign also provided multiple and concentrated opportunities for new leaders to emerge, and many with leadership in groups currently involved in the struggle for economic and social justice were new participants then. There was extensive contact across races and groups, and these interactions provided a foundation for a significant amount of current social action networking, mutual trust, and joint activity.

Finally, and perhaps most importantly, the Poor People's Campaign provided a dramatic voice for the many in America who are rarely heard. It changed and deepened their understanding of their situations, and it had a lifelong impact on many of them. It was a rare opportunity for oppressed people who were tired of the way things were, to try to do something about it.

Why then does the Poor People's Campaign still seem so amorphous, and why do I—and seemingly many others with whom I spoke—feel so ambivalent about the experience? Perhaps it is because the work that began then is still unfinished thirty years later. Today, in many communities it is difficult to perceive any remaining hope. The oppression of poverty seems inescapable, and agendas for change woefully ignored. For sure, we have yet to embrace the campaign's goal to confront and engage, even eradicate, the poverty among us. Yes, those directly involved in the Mule Train did find support for their hope and a renewed sense of themselves. For our own sakes, we must celebrate their legacy; to encourage the best in ourselves, we must honor what they as individuals, and the Poor People's Campaign as a movement, did. We must rekindle its passion for change and our conscience to deal with poverty.

This book is part of my personal rededication, my testimony to what the people of the Mule Train and the Poor People's Campaign—and the rest of us who were with them—did. Like the work we started then, this history is not complete, and I know I have missed some of the important linkages among the events of that summer. I can think of no greater tribute to emerge from this 30th Anniversary Celebration of the Mule Train than for others to move ahead with further clarification of what occurred, what we've learned, and what we must do as we move ahead. To me, that's the importance of "keeping hope alive." We must know what we did, what we achieved, and what it means. Most importantly, we must keep in our faces the bravery shown and the value of pulling others along.

APPENDIX

Roster of Mule Train Participants

This roster of participants is based on original records, developed while I was with the Mule Train. It includes those who started with us in Marks, Mississippi, as well as those who joined enroute. While perhaps not exact, the roster comes awfully close, at least as far as who was there through Birmingham, Alabama, where I left.

The list is based on registration cards filled out by passengers and collected by four volunteer recorders. The cards asked for a range of information about each person—including name, address, gender, age, role on the Mule Train, emergency contact, and the wagon in which traveling,—from which we've extracted what appears here. Not all cards were filled out completely, and in some cases individuals registered with more than one of the recorders. Though we've eliminated obvious duplications and filled in reasonable gaps, errors in the original data will also appear here. Also please note that roles on the Mule Train were fluid and often shared. See page 102—Marks to Atlanta—for additional infomration and analysis of the participant roster.

Name	City	S	Sex	Age	Role-In Addition to Passenger
Charles Alexander	Grenada	MS	M	18	
John Amos	Grenada	MS	M	17	
Roosevelt Archie	Memphis	TN	M	30	Wagon Driver
Doris Baker	Marks	MS	F	27	Volunteer Staff
Alexis Barrett	Birmingham	AL	F	17	
Willie Bolden	Atlanta	GA	M	28	Wagon Master/SCLC Staff
Tyrone Brooks	Social Circle	GA	M	22	SCLC Staff
Henry Lee Brown	Marks	MS	M	12	
Shirley (Jean) Brown	Holly Springs	MS	F	15	Assistant Recorder
Rev. John Burrell	Bessemer	AL	M	38	Volunteer Staff
James Roscoe Carthen	Brooklyn	NY	M	20	Wagon Driver
Joan Cashin	Huntsville	AL	F	32	Mule Train Organizer
John Cashin	Huntsville	AL	M	(30s)	Mule Train Organizer
Dave Catlin Jr.	Redwood	MS	M	42	
Rev. L. C. Coleman	Marks	MS	M	44	Wagon Driver
Jenette Collins	Marks	MS	F	11	
Kathleen Collins	Marks	MS	F	11	
Lee Dora Collins	Marks	MS	F	42	
Ida Collins	Marks	MS	F	13	
Shirley Jean Collins	Marks	MS	F	15	
Cable Common	Marks	MS	M	66	Wagon Driver
Myrtle Copeland	Huntsville	AL	F	(30s)	Mule Train Organizer
Dorothy Jean Corter	Tuscaloosa	AL	F	21	
Amos Crawford	Marks	MS	M	20	Wagon Driver
Emerald Theresa Cunningham	Grenada	MS	F	16	
Patricia Annette Tamika Deire	Grenada	MS	F	17	
Eugene Ellis	Chicago	IL	M	20	Wagon Driver
James W. Eskridge	Grenada	MS	M	19	Assistant Wagon Driver
Michael Faisom	Grenada	MS	M	18	Wagon Driver
Tyrom Figgs	Marks	MS	M	16	Assistant Wagon Driver
Clarence Franklin	Marks	MS	M	11	
Jessie Franklin	Marks	MS	M	51	Wagon Driver
Margaret Franklin	Marks	MS	F	13	
Ada Freeman	Chicago	IL	F	22	
Roland L. Freeman	Washington	D.C.	M	31	Photodocumentation Officer
Marion A. Gay	Grenada	MS	M	19	
Alex Ghoston	Winona	MS	M	20	
Dora LynLynn Ghoston	Winona	MS	F	20	Volunteer Staff
James Gibson	Atlanta	GA	M	22	
Phillip Goober	Atlanta	GA	M	28	Volunteer Staff
Clinton Albert Gordon	Duck Hill	MS	M	6	
Donald Dewayne Gordon	Duck Hill	MS	M	2	

Name	City	S	Sex	Age	Role-In Addition to Passenger
Mary Sue Gordon	Duck Hill	MS	F	25	
Sarah Louise Gordon	Duck Hill	MS	F	5	
Tommie Green		MS	M	18	
James Hall	Kilmichael	MS	M	16	Assistant Wagon Driver
Robert Lee Hall	Marks	MS	M	11	
Charles Hankins	Marks	MS	M	12	
Henry Hayes		MS	M	14	
Henry Haygood	Marks	MS	M	16	Wagon Driver
Charlie Heath	Waverly	FL	M	18	Assistant Wagon Driver
Charlie Heath	Marks	MS	M	19	Assistant Wagon Driver
Sadie Hill	Lambert	MS	F	18	Assistant Recorder
Lillian Hines		MS	F	13	
Minnie Holmes	Starkville	MS	F	53	
Margorie G. Hyatt	Pittsburgh	PA	F	21	
L. M. Jackson	Memphis	TN	M	22	Assistant Wagon Driver
Bertha M. Johnson	Marks	MS	F	28	Volunteer Staff
Brenda Johnson	Marks	MS	F	1 1/2	
Brenda Marie Johnson	Marks	MS	F	9	
Brian Micheal Johnson	Marks	MS	M	7	
Charles Milton Johnson Jr.	Marks	MS	M	8	
Dobbie Ann Johnson	Marks	MS	F	8 mos.	
Flossie Mae Johnson	Marks	MS	F	24	
Nelson Edward Johnson	Marks	MS	M	6	
Sylvia Johnson	Grenada	MS	F	15	
Terence Avery Johnson	Marks	MS	M	4	
Trudy Alane Johnson	Marks	MS	F	3	
Nathan Kepn	Marks	MS	M	15	Wagon Driver
Ida Mae Lloyd	Marks	MS	F	12	
Percy L. Manlow	Atlanta	GA	M	46	
Andrew Marrsett	Birmingham	AL	M	27	SCLC Staff
Denise Martin	Holly Springs	MS	F	13	Assistant Recorder
Emma Ruth Martin	Holly Springs	MS	F	35	
Jean Martin	Holly Springs	MS	F	14	
Percy Mayfield	Memphis	TN	M	18	Wagon Driver
Juanita Miller	Memphis	TN	F	26	Volunteer Staff
Willie Miller	Marks	MS	M	71	Wagon Driver
Bessie Monroe	Fayette	MS	F	53	
Jome Myer	Marks	MS	M	23	
Bobby Nelson	Atlanta	GA	M	27	SCLC Staff
Richard Palambo	Memphis	TN	M	16	
James Henry Parker	Grenada	MS	M	13	
William Parker	Grenada	MS	M	65	
Cecil Lee Payne		MS	F	13	
Emma L. Perry	Dorchester	MA	F	18	
Ray Poe	French Camp	MS	M	17	Assistant Wagon Driver
Lillie Poindexter	Columbus	MS	F	18	
Vincent Poindexter	Columbus	MS	M	2	
Faye Porche	Atlanta	GA	F	26	SCLC Staff
Annie V. Rankin	Fayette	MS	F	35	Assistant Wagon Driver
Evon Richmond	Lambert	MS	F	20	Volunteer Staff
Jesse L. Robertson		MS	M	24	Assistant Wagon Driver
William (Doug) Rubin	Memphis	TN	M	32	
Sylvester Sheffield	Atlanta	GA	M	28	SCLC Staff
George Shinhoster	Atlanta	GA	M	22	Volunteer Staff
James Speller	Windsor	NC	M	34	Volunteer Staff
Mary Will Tato	Winona	MS	F	21	Assistant Recorder
Willie E. Thomas	Marks	MS	M	56	Wagon Driver
Tommie Lee Tomas	Marks	MS	M	25	Wagon Driver
Lloyd Tratter	Holcomb	MS	M	23	Car and Truck Driver/SCLC Staff
James Travis Jr.	Grenada	MS	M	21	
Eddie Lee Webster	Lambert	MS	M	16	Assistant Wagon Driver
J. L. Wells	Atlanta	GA	M	22	Scout and Car Driver/SCLC Staff
Aaron Wilkins III	Holly Springs	MS	M	20	Wagon Driver
Allen Williams	Marks	MS	M	14	Assistant Wagon Driver
Bettye Williams	Grenada	MS	F	13	
Don E. (Joey) Williams	Memphis	TN	M	21	Volunteer Staff
Ellis Williams Jr.	Marks	MS	M	16	Wagon Driver
Hosea Williams	Atlanta	GA	M	(30's)	SCLC Staff
J.L. Williams	Atlanta	GA	M	23	SCLC Staff
Wilford Willis Jr.	Grenada	MS	M	26	Blacksmith/Muleskinner
Mack Woods		MS	M	74	Wagon Driver
Andrew Young	Atlanta	GA	M	36	SCLC Staff
Nalou C. (Unknown)	Grenada	MS	M	18	

Roland L. Freeman, self portrait
WASHINGTON, D.C., JULY 1997

ROLAND L. FREEMAN is a Washington, D.C.-based freelance photographer, whose work has been published widely and exhibited throughout the world, often along with quilts and other artifacts from his extensive collection of work by African-Americans. He is president of The Group for Cultural Documentation (TGCD), a publicly supported, tax-exempt organization, which he established in 1991 to contribute to the strength of our nation through the understanding, preserving, and bridging of cultural identities and traditions.

Freeman was the first photographer to be awarded a Young Humanist Fellowship by the National Endowment for the Humanities (1970). He has received two Masters of Photography Visual Arts Fellowships from the National Endowment for the Arts (1982, 1991), the Living Legend Award for Distinguished Achievement in Photography from the National Black Arts Festival (1994), and an Honorary Doctorate in Humane Letters from Millsaps College (Jackson, Mississippi, 1997).

A native of Baltimore, Maryland, Freeman began his professional career in the 1960s, photographing the Civil Rights movement. Assignments since then have emphasized photojournalism, commercial work, and photodocumentation. He has been a research photographer for the Smithsonian Institution's Center for Folklife Programs and Cultural Studies since 1972 and a faculty member at several universities.

A major emphasis of Freeman's work is his ongoing self-assigned project, *While There Is Still Time*, a study of black culture throughout the African Diaspora that uses the camera as a tool to research, document, and interpret the continuity of traditional African-American folklife practices. This work is generally done in close collaboration with folklorists, historians, sociologists, and community activists, often in methodologically innovative ways that have been integral to his contributions to the work of photographers of his generation.

Books by Freeman include: *Something To Keep You Warm: The Roland Freeman Collection of Black American Quilts from the Mississippi Heartland; Southern Roads/City Pavements: Photographs of Black Americans; Stand By Me: African American Expressive Culture in Philadelphia; The Arabbers of Baltimore; Margaret Walker's 'For My People': A Tribute, Photographs by Roland L. Freeman*; and *A Communion of the Spirits: African-American Quilters, Preservers, and Their Stories*, also published by Rutledge Hill Press. Each has been accompanied by a national/international touring exhibit.